WALKING IN LANCASHIRE

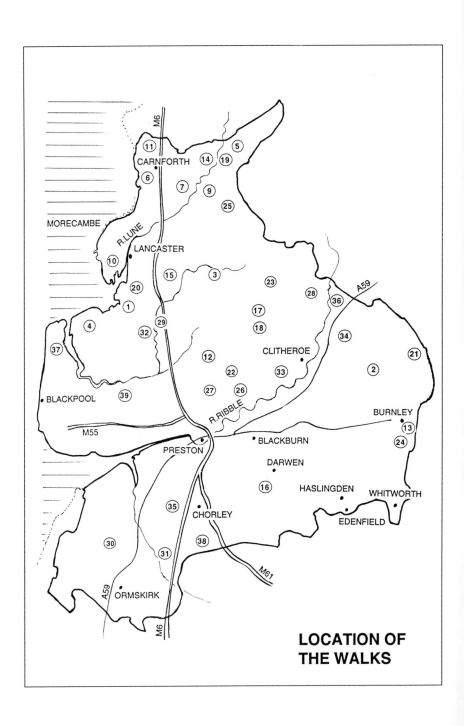

**LOCATION OF
THE WALKS**

WALKING IN LANCASHIRE

by

MARY WELSH

Illustrations by
DAVID MACAULAY &
LINDA WATERS

CICERONE PRESS
MILNTHORPE, CUMBRIA

ISBN 1 85284 191 5
A catalogue record for this book is available from the British Library.

ACKNOWLEDGEMENTS

Some walks have previously appeared in *Lancashire Life*; thanks to Brian Hargreaves, former editor, for his encouragement. Grateful thanks also go to my friend Maureen Fleming and to my daughter Cheryl. Both walked with me, researching and checking. Cami, my border collie, came too in the earlier walks but now, 16 years of age, she prefers a gentle stroll around the local pastures. Special thanks go to David Macaulay and Linda Waters for the drawings, which so enhance the text. Last but not least to Tom, my husband, for his unfailing support and advice.

Front Cover: Illustration by David Macaulay

CONTENTS

PREFACE

Advice to Readers

Readers are advised that whilst every effort is taken by the author to ensure the accuracy of this guidebook, changes can occur which may affect the contents. It is advisable to check locally on transport, accommodation, shops etc but even rights-of-way can be altered and, more especially overseas, paths can be eradicated by landslip, forest fires or changes of ownership.

The publisher would welcome notes of any such changes

PREFACE

Lancashire has a great variety of landscape. From the low lying land around Cockerham Abbey and Martin Mere to the heights of Darwen and Pendle Hill, the range is delightful.

It has a wealth of charming villages such as Aughton, Melling, Hurstwood, Dolphinholme, Nether Burrow, Chipping, Slaidburn, Ribchester, Bolton-by-Bowland, Downham, Croston and Sawley. Many have historical houses which have been lovingly maintained or faithfully restored and I hope the walker will enjoy these while passing by.

The circular walks are written according to the time of year, each emphasising the seasonal appeal of the landscape, the flora and the birds, although all the walks are right for any time of the year.

Lancashire is good walking country. But a word of caution: some walks take you over remote fells, through lonely glens or along quiet shores and the effects of rapid weather changes should not be underestimated. Go prepared with waterproofs, a map and extra food. Always wear suitable footwear. When crossing farmland stay on the right of way and follow the country code. Close gates, control dogs and respect the fences and walls of the hardworking farmers of this great county.

Good walking.

Dunsop Bridge (Walk 17)

1: Circular walk from Cockerham

Distance:	7½ miles
Time:	4 hours
Terrain:	Easy walking, some muddy farm tracks
Map:	OS Pathfinder 659 SD 45/55 Galgate and Dolphinholme

This walk leads you over quiet marshland pastures named after the hardworking farmers who reclaimed them from the sea. It allows you to watch the innumerable waders that feed in the Cocker Channel. It brings you to the remains of Cockersand Abbey, often wreathed in a sea mist that adds to its magical, mysterious atmosphere.

Park close to Cockerham parish hall, on the B5272, and take the signposted footpath to the north side of the hall. This is a wide reinforced track which leads to St Michael's church. The church has a solid ashlar-built Perpendicular tower, with the remainder built in 1910 by the famous architects Austin and Paley. Visit the churchyard and read the legends on the tombstones.

Leave by the kissing gate beyond the church, turn right and walk the path of paving stones to another gate to the road. Turn left and continue along the A588. Beyond the first cottage, cross the road and take a footpath, signposted Hillam, to a stile ahead that leads into a large flat pasture. Continue beside a ditch on the right to an attractive railed, wooden footbridge over a wider ditch. These ditches are a feature of the low-lying land and keep the rich pastures well drained. The footbridges too are another feature to note; pleasingly constructed, they enable you to cross the ditches safely.

Cross the next bridge, which is shadowed by a gnarled hawthorn. Walk ahead beside the ditch along a cart-track, and pass through a gate rather than the derelict stile that hangs over the ditch. Overhead a huge skein of geese, in V-formation, head for the marsh, calling noisily as they go. Continue to a stiled bridge over a dyke. Look left to see the buildings of the Black Knights parachute club.

Pass through some planted shrubs to a ladder stile over a fence. Turn left and continue to a stile over a fence. This leads to the access road to the parachute centre and Pattys Farm. Look back from the stile for a

good view of the church. Turn right and walk the track (part of the Lancashire Coastal Way) to the road. Away to the left stretch acres of marsh where shelduck feed in tidal gutters and curlews give their wild whistles and long, liquid bubbling calls.

Cross the road and turn left to walk along a high embankment. Here sheep feed from a molasses trough containing vitamin supplement, their faces stained dark brown. Oyster catchers fly overhead from the pastures on one side to the marsh on the other. A large flock of lapwings rise like a cloud and then settle to feed in another pasture. Stride ahead towards Bank End Farm and descend left to follow the coastal path signposted with a yellow waymark.

Pass the farmhouse and, where

St Michael's Church, Cockerham and Cockersand Abbey

10

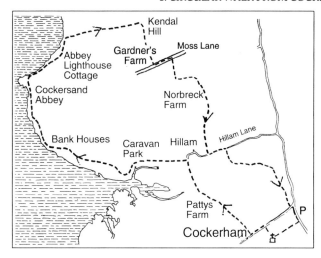

the track runs into the caravan site, keep to the left of the fence with the marsh and the Cocker Channel to your left. Enjoy the innumerable waders, busily feeding on the muddy edges of the river. Listen to the whistling calls of wigeon and teal and watch pairs of mallard rise. Step out along the raised embankment, past a row of gnarled hawthorn where fieldfares fly off with fast flight. Beyond in grassy pastures twenty or more swans graze.

Walk past the large caravan park at Bank Houses and continue ahead following the coastal way signpost. Now you have a first sighting of sand and bright red plates of sandstone close to the breakwater. Ahead, standing proud, is a lighthouse. Walk on until you come to a stile on the right. Beyond, where skylarks flit about the grass, walk to Cockersand Abbey, founded in 1190.

All that remains is the chapter house, two piles of stone and the atmosphere. Once it was a home for lepers and was approached over the sands when this part of Lancashire was a small island. The chapter house has crenellations and once was the burial chapel for the Dalton family who lived at Thurnham.

Return to the coastal path and continue ahead. Walk the high level flood wall path as it swings right. Pass through a kissing gate and continue to Abbey Lighthouse Cottage beside another lighthouse. An earlier lighthouse on this site was built of wood. The woman keeper used to climb the steps each day to replenish the paraffin to keep the light burning.

Continue along the coastal path. Notice the large number of redshanks which probe the mud trapped by the spartina grass on the shore. Just beyond the next cottage take the grey metal gate on the right. Continue ahead through the next gate and walk on to a footbridge. Look for long-legged hares here. Climb the fence ahead and look right to see Tomlinson's Farm and Clarkson's Farm, both named after the early reclaimers. Continue ahead over another stile and a footbridge to climb the slope to a stile to Kendal Hill Farm.

Turn right to pass through the farm buildings and then bear left, following a wide concrete track to pass behind the farm to a gate on the right. Stride the track (south) towards Gardner's Farm, keeping the ditch to the right. Pass through the green gate and walk ahead to the stile to the left of the farm buildings. A stile gives access to Moss Lane, where you turn left. Walk the hedged lane to pass the next building on the left, Haresnape's Farm, and continue to the footbridge on the right, signposted Hillam.

As you walk ahead, keeping beside the hedge, notice the drumlins, rounded hummocks of glacial material, a pleasing feature after so much flat land. At the boundary hedge, climb the stile on the left and walk ahead to cross five ditches, two of which have footbridges. Just beyond the second bridge look for the stile on the right, reached by stepping over a low barbed-wire fence. Beyond, walk ahead and then bear left to join a farm track that climbs right, past a small pond, to Norbreck Farm.

Walk through the farm buildings and bear right in front of a white house. Take the field gate opposite to the attractive dwelling and walk ahead over two pastures, where dozens of curlews feed, to Hillam Farm. Pass through the cobbled yard to Hillam Lane and turn left. Walk 400 yards to the gate on the right. Beyond, walk the cart-track, which is ditched on either side. Pass through the next gateway and turn left, keeping beside the ditch on the left. Cross the waymarked footbridge in the left corner of the pasture.

Strike slightly right to pass through two gates and then to a stile to the left of a building. Walk behind the dwelling to join an access track. Follow it as it swings right. Where it swings left walk ahead to a stile. Beyond climb the slope, keeping beside the hedge. Look right to see mixed woodland, the first on this mainly marshland walk. Climb a ladder stile to pass through a builder's yard and along a wide track to the A588. Cross and turn left into Cockerham. Pass in front of the Manor public house and continue to the car park.

2: Circular walk via Pendle Hill

Distance:	6 miles
Time:	3-4 hours
Terrain:	Steep climb to Pendle Beacon. Walking boots essential. Moorland paths could be wet after rain
Map:	OS Landranger 103 Blackburn, Burnley and surrounding area
Car Park and Refreshments:	Barley

Pendle Hill (1,831 feet) dominates the landscape for miles around. Its great whaleback shape broods over the attractive villages of Barley, Downham, Roughlee, Twiston and Newchurch, all set in glorious Lancashire countryside. Closely associated with the hill are the Pendle witches; ten, all of whom lived on farms and in the villages about the hill, were sent to the scaffold at Lancaster and at York in 1612. But not all the associations of the hill are fearsome; it was Pendle Hill that inspired George Fox to found the Quaker movement.

Park in the attractive picnic site close by the stream at Barley, north-west of Barrowford. Turn right and right again to walk past Pendle Inn and the Barley Mow. Turn left opposite the Methodist church to walk the signposted Pendle Way beside a dancing brook. Cross a stile and follow the well walked path through rough pastures. Step across a footbridge and turn left to continue beside the small stream. Continue along a metalled road with the beck now to your left.

Turn right through a signposted kissing gate to walk a fenced path. Fieldfare, with slate-grey heads and rumps, fly off from tall ash trees, uttering their harsh flight call. Continue past a large pond where a man and a heron, both fishers, sit quite still, hoping for a catch. Stride on beneath ash, alder, sycamore and hawthorn now bereft of leaves. These, bronzed and curled, litter the way and rustle as you continue on your walk. Pass through the signposted gate and walk ahead to cross a track. Carry on in the direction of the hill, following the white arrow and the painted word 'Pendle'.

Pendle Hill

Head along the narrow path to a signposted stile and on to a gate in the wall ahead. A flock of grouse rise with a startling whirr, to fly low over the vegetation. Look for the signposted stile on the right, just before the next wall. Beyond, walk ahead to pass in front of Pendle House. Away to the right lie the two Black Moss reservoirs, the upper completed in 1894 and the lower in 1903.

Continue to cross the cattle grid and then take the signposted gate on the left. Carry on to the kissing gate. From here starts the long stony path, ladder-like, that seems to lead almost to heaven. In fact, the reinforced way climbs steeply upwards almost to the top of the hill. It is well constructed and of local stone which blends with the slopes. Pause regularly - to catch your breath, to savour the magnificent views and to enjoy the wonderful peace.

Eventually the rusty red dead bracken that clothed the lower slopes is left behind and then the track becomes a rough stony way. Turn left before the wall that strides across the top and walk towards the beacon. The indistinct path crosses rough grass and bilberry where in summer

14

dotterel and wheatears haunt the peat hags. Look also for curlews, over-wintering meadow pipits and golden plover. The views from the summit are superb - what a pity there is no indicator panel to help with naming the many hills you can see.

Walk on from the beacon, keeping the Black Moss reservoirs to your left. Several large cairns denote the path. Where two paths stretch ahead keep to the one on the left (having now left the Pendle Way) with Lower Ogden reservoir coming into view. Continue along the narrow stony path and follow it as it begins the long descent towards the reservoir. Pass through the stile at the path end and climb another immediately to the left. Turn right and follow the wall down the slope to reach the access road to Higher Buttock Farm which has a striking wind pump.

Follow the road as it drops downhill and then turn right following the Pendle Way. Walk to the metal gate and climb the slope beyond. Turn left to cross the bridge between the two Ogden reservoirs and climb the stepped way to the signposted footpath. The path climbs over

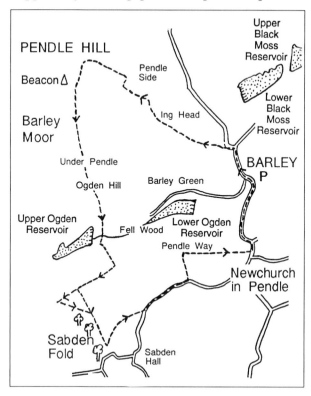

moorland to come close to a fence. At the waymarked stile in the fence, leave the Way and turn right to walk a grassy path between rushes to a stile. Continue ahead to a stone stile. Do not cross, but walk downhill, keeping to the left of a treeless gill. The indistinct path continues to a ruined building. From then on a good path drops downhill, keeping to the east side of the gill, its steep slopes densely wooded with magnificent beeches.

At the end of the wood, strike left to a ladder stile in the corner of the pasture. Beyond, strike diagonally left, climbing the slope. To the right lies a quiet valley with sturdy farmhouses scattered about the rolling pastures. The path leads to a narrow lane. Turn left and walk in the direction of Newchurch. Pass a white dwelling on the left and continue to the cattle-grid and entrance to the next house, Higher Wellhead Cottage. Pass through the white metal gate opposite and climb uphill to a gateless gap. Walk ahead again to a fence. Turn right here to rejoin the Pendle Way to walk beside the fence to a waymarked stile. Below, to the left, lies the head of Ogden reservoir and across the valley you can see the steep path you climbed to reach the top of Pendle Hill.

Continue ahead to a stone stile at the wall end. Beyond, carry on beside the hawthorn hedge to a stile at the end of it. Turn left to pass through a gap stile to the road. Walk downhill to Barley. As you enter the village look left to see a waterworks building. This has been built on the site of a cotton mill, one of five that thrived in the valley. This one was washed away in a great storm of 1880. After that the flood waters of the wayward river were harnessed with the building of the Ogden reservoirs.

3: Circular walk in Wyresdale

Distance:	6 miles
Time:	3-4 hours
Terrain:	Easy walking for most of the way. Can be muddy. Walking boots advisable
Maps:	OS Pathfinder 659 SD 45/55 Galgate and Dolphinholme
	660 SD 65/75 Slaidburn and Forest of Bowland

This is just the walk to help you keep to your new year resolution to take more exercise; also your second resolution, to see more of Lancashire - and, I will be brave and add, Lancashire at its best. The walk takes you beside two glorious becks, the Marshaw Wyre and the Tarnbrook Wyre, and skirts the rolling moors as you go.

Just east of Abbeystead reservoir and the hamlet of Abbeystead, cross Stoops Bridge and turn right into a public road. Park in a grassy area beside the Marshaw Wyre. Walk on along the lane and turn left to begin the well waymarked and signposted route. Pass through peaceful deciduous woodland to a gate into a pasture. Continue ahead to a gate to the left of a shed. Look left to see Abbeystead, the magnificent mansion of the Duke of Westminster, who owns all the land over which this walk passes. With tongue in cheek, a local described it as the Duke's country cottage.

Cross the beck by a wooden footbridge and continue ahead with the hurrying water to your left and woodland to your right. As you climb you have a sudden pleasing glimpse of Hawthornthwaite Fell, and here you must promise yourself a walk this way when the tops are purple with heather. Look for the waymarks on the fence beside a small copse, which now lies between you and the Marshaw. At the next kissing gate pause and look down into a charming hollow where the lovely river makes a sharp loop.

Continue into more woodland and look for a stone marker telling you that the trees were planted in 1908 when Lord Sefton was the owner of Abbeystead. Beyond the next stile, descend the steps to cross a small stream. Then the path skirts left of a grassy bluff to come close to the lively beck once more. Continue straight ahead, where the Wyre makes

another large loop to cross a footbridge. Here is a sheltered corner to dawdle, where gorse is nearly always in bloom and long tailed tits slip elegantly through the treetop branches.

Beyond, climb the slope, and ahead lie Hawthornthwaite Fell and Marshaw Fell. The way lies close to the fence on your right, coming beside the beck once more. Ignore the stile on the right and straddle the stile and cross the footbridge ahead. Walk beside the woodland on your left and stride across the pasture to a

ladder stile to the road. (If you are following the Pathfinder map, the right of way seems to have been changed - do not climb the wall but keep to the left of the hedge.)

Stroll along the beech lined road. If the traffic is intrusive you might wish to take the stile over the wall on the right, which is topped with a white waymark, to continue in the same direction, keeping beside the beck. Close to Marshaw the beck has washed away the path but if the water is not high, convenient stones at the edge of the water help. This small diversion ends

Wooden bridge over River Wyre with gorse in bloom

18

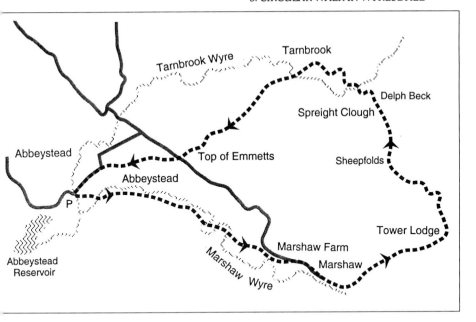

with a ladder stile over a boundary wall. Overhead, a pair of kestrels hover in hunt of prey. Continue between oaks and pines until you reach Tower Lodge to take the waymarked footpath on the left, just before the dwelling.

Begin the gradual ascent of the stony track. Look back for a good view of the moors and the skirt of pines which softens their harshness. Pass through a gate into the high pastures and follow the waymark on your left, directing you diagonally right to pass through the ruined wall on your right. Continue in the same direction to a ladder stile over the fence. Here Dunkenhaw Fell comes into view, sloping upwards, bleak and harsh, towards Ward's Stone.

Keeping in the same direction, carry on to climb a metal ladder stile. Beyond, turn right and drop down the slope, to pass through a gate to the left of two sheepfolds in the right corner of the pasture. From here, left, you can see Morecambe Bay, stretching away westwards, silvery-blue in the winter sunshine. Head on down the pasture, with tall beeches over the wall on your right, to a gate. Pass through and press on downhill. Look over the wall to see the immensely deep trench of Spreight Clough. Pass through yet another gate and the next which gives access to a farm-track that passes over a cobbled yard between two barns. Cross a small stone bridge and then a larger one to follow the track towards a farm. Follow the clear waymarks to skirt the dwelling to cross the Tarnbrook Wyre by a footbridge on your right.

Stride the farm-track, from where you can hear grouse uttering their familiar 'Go back, go back' call. Pass through the gate to a farmyard and the quiet little cluster of houses at Tarnbrook, a dead end for cars. Once there were twenty-five dwellings and the menfolk made felt hats and gloves. After a hundred yards, look left to see the footpath leading off left, under a Scots pine. Beyond the gate, walk the walled track to cross the footbridge over the brook.

Stride the way to the ladder stile and then on along the grassy track to a waymarked gate. Head slightly right to a stile to the right of a gate. Continue to the next stile, and then to the next, in the opposite hedge. Cross a narrow track to the next ladder stile. Stroll on in the same direction, with the fence to your left, to a stone stile in the left corner. Carry on, passing a barn on your right, to a ladder stile into rough pasture. Here, after a big step across a ditch, press on with the wall to your right. When it swings right, continue ahead to a stile in the left corner by a fence. Turn left and walk to the next ladder stile. Beyond, turn right and walk beside the hedge to the stile to the access track to Top of Emmetts Farm. Turn left and walk to the road, which you cross.

Beyond the waymarked stile, bear right towards a waymarked telegraph pole. Keep ahead, with a fence and a ditch to the right. Pass through a gate and carry on slightly left to a ladder stile in the left corner into the garden of a cottage. Walk to the road and turn left. Descend the hill, with a pleasant glimpse of the reservoir through the trees. Pass the lodge to Abbeystead and continue to the parking area at Stoops Bridge.

4: Circular walk from Knott End

Distance:	5½ miles
Time:	2-3 hours
Terrain:	Easy walking all the way
Map:	OS Pathfinder 658 SD 34/35 Fleetwood
Refreshments:	Knott End Cafe

This is a wonderfully invigorating walk for a bright winter's day. It takes you beside the wide, silvery estuary of the River Wyre, continues through quiet pastures hedged with trees whose buds are still tightly closed, continues past well kept fishing ponds and a teeming duck farm and returns you along Knott End Esplanade, with extensive views over Morecambe Bay.

Park in the car park, behind Knott End Cafe, once the terminus for the 'Pilling Pig', the old Garstang to Knott End railway. The cafe stands at the western end of the esplanade, overlooking the point where the River Wyre surges out into Morecambe Bay. Walk upstream of the river (with the estuary to your right) along the signposted footpath, with the pleasing skyline of Fleetwood across the water on the opposite bank. Oyster catchers, redshank and shelduck probe in the tidal gutters.

Just before the Sea Dyke Cottage (1754), turn left away from the estuary path. Turn right behind the dwelling to follow the footpath as it swings right, along the edge of the golf course, where gorse is in bloom. Follow the path and then, with care, the waymarks directing you diagonally left across the links to join a farm-track. Continue right, past a pond, part-edged with willows. Follow the waymark to turn left into Whinny Lane. Stroll through ash, sycamore and elm to pass the Jacobean Hackensall Hall. Stride on, ignoring all turns, past a small lake where rhododendrons grow, out into the pastures. As you pass a wet area, where the dead wands of Great Reed rustle in the wind, look for a heron waiting patiently for prey.

At the junction of tracks turn right to walk the bed of the old railway, which is lined with wintry hedgerows. The way passes through a small wood and more pastures. Ignore the right turn and continue to an opening onto Hall Gate Lane, which you cross and turn right. Continue

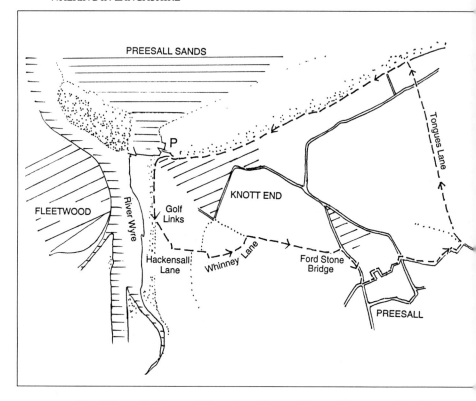

over Ford Stone Bridge and into the village of Preesall to pass the Black Bull and the Saracen's Head on your right.

Turn left into Smithy Lane and left again in front of Preesall's Charity School. Turn left once more, behind the garage of the house on your left, to walk the winding fenced path around the school's nature trail. From here there are splendid views of the Fylde Plain and the Forest of Bowland beyond.

Before the end of the fenced way, look out for the stile on your left. It gives access to sloping ground, which you descend to a footbridge over a ditch. Stride on to cross two stiles and then a ladder stile to a road. Cross, turn left and then right into Gaulters Lane, a hedged track that leads into the flat pastures beyond Preesall. Look for the fascinating small windmill in the grounds of a ruined building.

At the end of the lane, just before the gate, turn left to walk a signposted narrow strip of grass between a ditch and the fence of a cottage. Pass through a kissing gate and a gate to a pasture. Cross this on a right diagonal to a footbridge over another ditch. Look here for skylarks, oyster catchers and green plovers. Walk ahead to a broken stile below two scrubby hawthorns. Beyond, continue between two fishing ponds (Boubles ponds), the haunt of coot, to join a lane where you turn left.

Stride on until you come to another pond, where you turn right into the gated and stiled Tongues Lane, a private road with footpath access. The flat treeless pastures stretch away on either side. Ignore the footpath on the left and right and dawdle past the duck farm where hundreds of pairs are reared. When the lane swings sharp right, round the end of the duck pens, walk ahead along a narrow path between a ditch to your left and a building on your right to a rickety footbridge. Carry on to a stile into a paddock and another out of it and on to a signposted stile to Pilling Lane, which you cross.

Pass through another stile and walk the stiled path, with the ditch to your right, to the steps up to the embankment. Turn left and walk the breezy path, where huge limestone boulders have been piled high as part of the sea defence. From the path you can see Black Combe and the continuing line of the Lakeland hills. Barrow's submarine shed rears tall and white out over the waters of the bay. The pleasing path returns you to Knott End and the esplanade. Head on to the car park, where you started the walk.

Promenade, Knott End

5: Circular walk from Kirkby Lonsdale, including Whittington

Distance:	4¹⁄₂ miles
Time:	2-3 hours
Terrain:	Easy walking all the way
Maps:	OS Pathfinder 628 SD 67/68 Kirkby Lonsdale and Barbon
	637 SD 56/57 Burton-in-Kendal and Caton

What better way to spend a winter's day than to walk beside a stately river, look across rolling pasture to a spectacular hill, visit a quiet Lancashire village and observe an abundance of bird life? All this can be enjoyed on a circular walk from Kirkby Lonsdale.

Park in the large parking area by the Devil's Bridge, on the north side of the A65. Take the stone steps down to the path beside the River Lune, on the south-west side of the magnificent bridge, which dates from the fourteenth century. Enjoy its graceful twin arches and the legend about its name. It is said that an old woman whose cow and pony strayed across the river promised the devil that if he raised a bridge so that her stock could cross the river, he could have the first thing that crossed. Early next morning the old woman's mangy dog ran over the bridge after a bun thrown by the old woman. The devil, expecting he would gain a pony or a cow, vanished in angry flames.

Continue along the footpath beside the surging water, walking beneath oak, hawthorn and elm. Pass through the kissing gate just before the next bridge and walk up the slope to the A65. Cross the busy road and walk down stone steps to regain the footpath to continue downstream. Seagulls circle overhead and mallards call from the shallows. A flock of pied wagtails collect on a drystone wall before their flight south.

The next bridge carries great pipes for the water board over the Lune. After passing under the bridge bear to the right and ascend a small embankment to climb an awkward stile. Then pass through a squeeze stile and in a few yards take another stile on the left to steps leading once more to the riverside.

A lively flock of blue tits fly upstream and settle in an overhanging

alder, whispering quietly to each other.
Walk on along a wide grassy terrace
with a copse of sycamore, ash and oak
to the right. Stride along the continuing
narrow path, hedged with layered
hawthorn, that rises above the lovely
river, with rolling pasture stretching
away on either side.

Look to the left for a magnificent

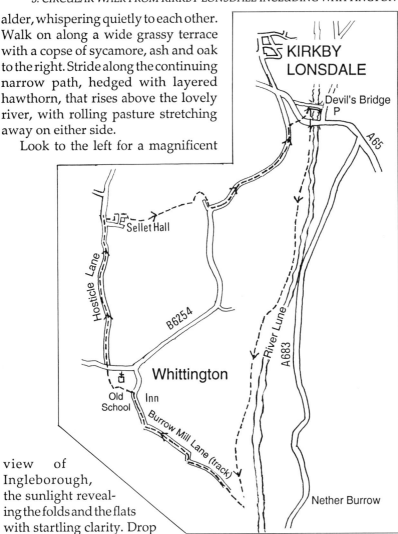

view of
Ingleborough,
the sunlight reveal-
ing the folds and the flats
with startling clarity. Drop
down a short slope to climb a
rickety stile. At the water's edge a dipper runs into the shallows and
then back to a shingle reach.

Continue along the way, bearing to the right to cross a small feeder
beck. In hawthorns, dozens of fieldfares - large grey-headed thrushes -
feed on a few remaining berries. Stride the stiled way and just before a
wooden hut on the riverbank climb the stile to the left of a metal gate.

Fieldfare

Straddle the next stile and then descend the three-stepped ladder to walk in front of a wooden hut. Continue a short way along the riverbank until you reach a gate on your right. Beyond, bear slightly right to pass through a signposted gate to a farm track, Burrow Mill Lane. Stroll on between hedges of holly, bramble, hawthorn and ash. Look ahead to the Church of St Michael the Archangel, with the houses and cottages of Whittington gathered around it. The track, very muddy in places after rain, passes Low Hall Farm and then comes to the B6254.

Turn right to walk through the attractive village. Cross the road and take the walled track beyond an old school, now housing a builders' merchant. Continue across the meadows, passing through several gates to climb the steps to the church on its hill. Here you may care to sit in one of the lovely oak pews and meditate.

Walk on and leave the churchyard by the north gate. Turn left and then in 10 yards take the sheltered, narrow lane, Hosticle Lane, on the right, climbing steeply uphill in the direction of Sellet Hall. The lane is walled and supports, in places, a hedge 6 feet high. At the top of the slope, look right for another grand view of Ingleborough. Just beyond a small wood on the right is an enclosed pond from where come the calls of pochards, shelduck and mallards. Continue on a dozen yards and take a right turn, signposted Shellet Hall Herb Garden and Action Learning Centre. Continue through the car park and onto a cart-track. Pass through a gate. It appears to be locked, but if you manoeuvre it carefully, extending a long chain, you can continue along the way. Bear left and follow the hedge downhill to a waymarked gate on the left.

Beyond, walk ahead to another waymarked gate. Pass through and turn right to walk to a signposted gate on the right. Take the ornate white gate opposite and walk down past several dwellings. Look left to see the three-storeyed house, Sellet Mill, with its water wheel. At the B6254 turn left and walk towards Kirkby Lonsdale. Notice the limekiln just beside the mill.

At one point along the road you are in a no-man's-land, the gap between the Lancashire boundary and the Cumbria boundary sign. Just beyond the electricity sub-station, set among trees, turn right to take a small gate onto pasture. Walk left to the kissing gate onto the A65. Cross the road to take another kissing gate. Walk across the meadow to the stone steps to the car park.

6: Circular walk from Yealand Conyers via Leighton Hall and Leighton Moss, returning over Warton Crag

Distance:	5 miles
Time:	3 hours (more if time is spent in the hide)
Terrain:	Easy walking on the grass, woodland paths and on a road. Always wise to wear walking boots
Maps:	OS Pathfinder 637 SD 56/57 Burton-in-Kendal 636 SD 37/47 Grange-over-Sands

This walk takes you through a quiet corner of north-west Lancashire. It comes close to a stately home surrounded by gracious parkland, where, in spite of the snow, young lambs frolic. It passes through a nature reserve where coot take off, uncertainly, from frozen meres. It returns you over the peaceful wooded slopes of Warton Crag.

Start at Yealand Conyers, a linear village of gracious houses, just off the A6, 2½ miles north of Carnforth. Park in the yard of the New Inn, where the owner welcomes walkers. Walk uphill to the stone stile on your right, opposite The Old Post House. Head up the lightly snow-dusted grassy slope, beyond, to cross the private access road to Yealand Manor. Continue ahead, as directed by the footpath sign, to a squeeze stile in the facing wall.

A faint path (signposted) leads a few yards left, and then right, up the slope through beech and sweet chestnut to another gap stile. Continue ahead to the right of a large stepped cairn of limestone to pass through a gate in the facing wall. Walk beneath stately beech and sycamore, their trunks still coated with snow, to a convenient seat. Pause here and enjoy the magnificent view.

Below lies Leighton Hall, owned by Major and Mrs Reynolds, descendants of the Gillows (of furniture fame). Its history started in 1246 as a fortified manor on land granted to Adam D'Avranches by William de Lancaster, Baron of Kendal in 1173. In 1763 George Townley had the house rebuilt in Adam style, the park laid out and the woods

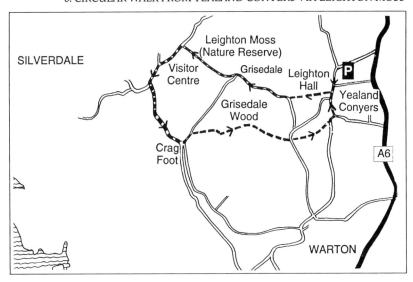

replanted. Beyond lie the reed-fringed meres of Leighton Moss nature reserve. In the distance you can see Arnside Knott and the waters of the Kent Estuary.

Drop downhill, over the pastures with their sheep and lambs, to the private road to the Hall. Turn right and walk past the side of the Hall and then along a hedged lane from which there are grand views of the snow covered tops of the Lakeland hills. At Grisedale Farm follow the signposted track that swings right to the gated entrance to the causeway across Leighton Moss. The reserve lies in a wooded valley, its limestone floor covered with marine clay, overlaid with peat. Water from the surrounding hills drains into the valley and forms three main meres. About these grow extensive reed beds which have to be controlled to prevent them encroaching upon the open water.

Stroll along the track between the tall reeds, which sway and whisper in the chilly March wind. Listen for the sharp metallic call of a bearded tit and the indifferent song of the handsome male reed bunting. From the public hide watch tufted duck, pochard, wigeon and coot, all enjoying a small area of the mere. Look also for the bittern that crouches between the dead and broken reeds of winter, occasionally filling the air with its boom.

Continue along the causeway and turn left onto the road to Silverdale. Continue to the Visitor Centre, where you may like to browse in the shop. Close to the car park look for the marsh tits feeding on the nuts hanging in a bag on a tree. At the road junction, turn left into Slackwood Lane. Take the next left to cross the level crossing. Walk on to Quicksand Pool Bridge, just before the hamlet of Crag Foot. (This road walking - less than a mile - is unavoidable.)

At Crag Foot turn left. On the right towers the chimney of an old steam pump. Until 1917 it was linked with dykes that drained the moss so that it could be used for agriculture. Walk along the wide cart-track and turn right, just before the farm on the left. After 20 yards turn left into ash woodland, as directed by a sign. Walk the narrow path to pass through a gap stile into a clearing. Continue ahead to take a gate on the right, just before the boundary wall. (The footpath sign lies beyond the gate.)

Walk the wide limestone track to take the left of two gates. Here a pair of bullfinches call quietly from the birch and ash copse to your left. Stride along the way, keeping the woodland to your left, to a gate with

". . . the bittern that crouches . . between
broken reeds of winter" Leighton Moss

two stiles. Follow the waymark, pointing slightly to the right, towards a sturdy oak with a large footpath sign. Another waymark is fixed to a sycamore tree just ahead, directing you right, to a thin path up the wooded slope to a stone style (difficult to find when the trees are in leaf).

Beyond, follow the track, keeping to the stone wall to your left. Pass through a gate and continue along the wide track (Green Lane) beside glorious deciduous woodland from where a green woodpecker flies off across the pastures on the left. At the track end, cross the road and pass through the waymarked stile opposite. Walk ahead, following the clear track to pass through a gateless gap. Continue along the good path, steadily dropping downhill past a magnificent limekiln on the left.

Stride onwards, with more woodland to the right, part of the Woodland Trust where the public are invited to walk. Look for the waymark on a lofty Scots pine to help you on your way. Continue downhill and follow the faint path left to a wobbly stile to the road. Turn left and walk through the village of Yealand Conyers, from where there is a magnificent view to another snowy hill, Ingleborough. Continue downhill to the New Inn.

7: Circular walk from the Crook of Lune

Distance:	7 miles
Time:	3-4 hours
Terrain:	Easy walking all the way
Map:	OS Pathfinder 637 SD 56/57 Burton-in-Kendal & Caton

The Lune is perhaps the finest of Lancashire's rivers. It rises in Cumbria and then idles through its fertile valley with a series of graceful meanders. In March its waters resound to the calls of waders and ducks, its banks colourful with celandines and kingcups, its trees laden with catkins. Its quiet peacefulness is broken only by the loud splash of a leaping salmon.

Leave your car in the pleasing parking area sited above the neck of the great bend in the river - the Crook of Lune. In 1835 William Wordsworth praised its loveliness and the beauty spot was a must for all nineteenth century travellers. William Turner was inspired to paint a water colour which now hangs in the Courtauld Institute in London. Twentieth century walkers will find the Crook a magnificent start for a walk.

Drop down the good path to the riverside and take the footpath, signposted Loyn Bridge, where celandines flower and ramsons and bluebells push dark green leaves through the still wintry ground. Notice the five-arched bridge, with its splendid wrought-iron balustrade, spanning the surging river, which used to carry the railway from Green Ayre, Lancaster, to Wennington. Stroll to a waymarked gate and continue beside the hurrying water.

Look across the river to see the eighteenth century Caton Low Mill, which produced cotton until the 1970s. Follow the well waymarked way where willow carries silver buds and larch is adorned with 'pink roses', the female flowers. Curlews call from the pastures and a shelduck flies downstream. A stepped path takes you above the river, passing through deciduous woodland. Here in wet flushes grow great numbers of the tiny-flowered golden saxifrage.

Pass the ornate three-arched waterworks bridge and take the waymarked stile into Applehouse Wood. Here chaffinches are in full song and an early willow warbler practises his sweet spring warble.

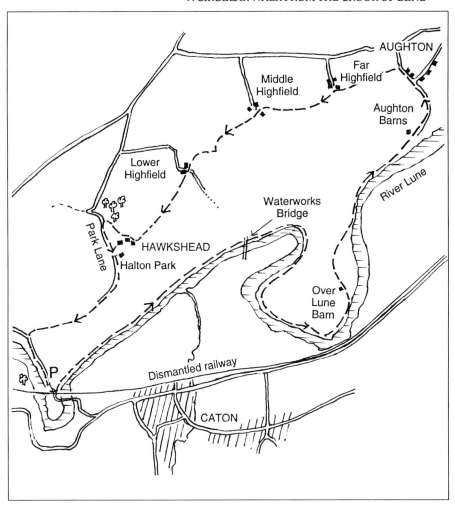

Climb the stile out of the trees and follow the well waymarked path that runs beside the Lune where it makes a large horseshoe-shaped meander. Here the walker should dawdle, enjoying to the full the noisy, restless oyster catchers, the melodious redshanks and the wheeling and diving green plovers.

Look for the waymark that directs you left, away from the river, to walk to the right of Over Lune Barn and on to the stile ahead. Beyond, the way continues right, slightly raised, across a large pasture to come

". . . picturesque golden-brown stone houses . . ."

to the side of the waymarked Lune once more. Straddle the stile to the side of a gate across a reinforced track, to the left of a wooden hut. Here kingcups brighten a dark corner of a pasture. Follow the track as it swings left in front of the farmhouse, Aughton Barns. Here leave the footpath beside the Lune to continue on the track. It soon becomes a narrow tree-lined lane and climbs steeply to the hamlet of Aughton.

As you toil uphill enjoy the primroses, wood anemones and barren strawberry that flower beneath the burgeoning hawthorn, elder and honeysuckle. At the lane end there is a seat where you can recover your breath and look at the picturesque golden-brown stone houses. Continue ahead from the lane up the hill to a signposted footpath on the left. Notice the sturdy iron ladder stile, the first of many that you climb as you walk the airy way high above the river.

Keep to the left of High Barn to another stile, then, bearing slightly diagonally left, climb a large pasture full of sheep with lambs, to another stile in the boundary fence. From here look back to see Hornby Castle.

Stride on to cross the footbridge to a stile to the left of Far Highfield. Walk ahead, with the fence to your right, to another stile, and on to the next with a hedge to your right. Stroll the stiled way beside the hedge to Middle Highfield.

A stile gives access to a paddock with caravans. Cross and climb the stile to the right of a gate to pass in front of the farm. Pass through the gate on the left and take a stone stile on the right in front of a building that was once a chapel. Walk a cobbled way to descend stone steps. Turn left and walk to pass through a gate beyond a large farm building where you turn right. Bear right until you see a high wall on your right.

Follow the track to a metal gate and head on, by the wall, to the next gate. Pass through and stride across the narrow pasture to the gate ahead. Beyond, walk across to the boundary, where you turn left and walk to Lower Highfield. Continue left along a farm track, following it as it swings right towards the farm. At this point you can see the footpath sign painted on a wall.

Follow the track down the slope, take the right of two gates, cross a tiny stream to a gate and then walk ahead to a waymarked kissing gate into pleasing woodland. Leave the trees by another kissing gate and walk ahead close beside a hedge on your right. Look out for the footpath bordered by a low wall which leaves the hedge, right, just before the dwellings at Hawkshead. Drop down the slope to a stile to a track along which you walk right to Park Lane. Turn left and carry on along the quiet lane, past the gracious Halton Park, until you reach Low Road. Turn left and, with care, walk back to rejoin your car.

8: Circular walk around Whalley

Distance:	5¹/₂ miles
Time:	3 hours
Terrain:	Easy walking most of the way. Steepish climb out of Whalley
Map:	OS Pathfinder 680 SD 63/73 Longridge and Great Harwood

The picturesque ruins of Whalley Abbey stand among trees in a glorious sheltered valley. Close by is the ancient church of St Mary's. This March walk visits both and continues through the peaceful Lancashire countryside, where spring is just beginning.

The aptly named Spring Wood picnic site provides ample parking. It lies on the east side of the A671, the Whalley Easterly by-pass, less than half a mile from the village itself. Return to the dual carriageway and cross. Ascend the unmarked footpath, which climbs up the slope beneath hawthorn and rowan from which great tits call. Coltsfoot flowers about the path.

Beyond the trees bear right across the pasture, keeping parallel with the fenced woodland to your right. Look left to see the Whalley Arches, a brick-built viaduct of thirty-two arches which once carried the Blackburn-to-Chatburn railway. Continue down the sloping pasture to a stile. Beyond, cross a small, muddy field to another stile to a reinforced track. Turn left and walk on, enjoying the wood anemones and celandines that flourish in the hedgerow, into Whalley.

Cross the main road and walk on along Station Road. Take the second turn on the left, Abbey Road, and continue on the footpath that takes you across Abbots Way play area to a kissing gate onto the road. Walk ahead towards the turreted gatehouse to visit Whalley Abbey. Wander through the lovely grounds and the roofless cloisters. The abbey belonged to the Cistercian order. Though no picture exists of the original abbey, finished in the 1440s, the ruins and records give the impression of a magnificent building.

Return beneath the gatehouse and follow the road right to pass through The Square. Look left to see some ancient buildings once used to store fishing equipment for the abbey. On the right stands the parish church of St Mary. Pause in the churchyard to view the Celtic crosses, possibly dating from the tenth century, and the many old gravestones.

The building of the present church began about 1200. Allow yourself plenty of time to enjoy the lovely building. Look for the Catterall Brass and marvel at the couple's twenty children. Visit the exquisitely carved choir stalls, originally made for the abbey and installed in the church after the dissolution.

Return to Church Lane, a continuation of The Square, and walk to King Street. Turn right and walk past the shops to cross Whalley Bridge over the River Calder. Cross the road and begin the steepish climb up Moor Lane. After 100 yards, where the road swings right, bear left, climbing a reinforced path below magnificent beech trees. At a strategically placed seat for enjoying the magnificent view, take the right-hand walled bridlepath to continue climbing.

When you reach the edge of a beech wood, turn right, keeping to the

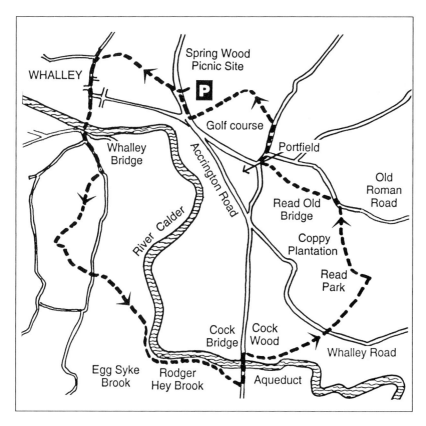

left of a fenced pasture. Walk beneath more beeches, through which flit long tailed tits, to a stile. Cross the track beyond and straddle the stile to continue climbing beneath more beech. Walk on, keeping beside the fence to your left and following it as it swings left to an easy-to-miss stile into the garden of a house. Immediately take the stile on your left, out of the garden and walk right to another stile back into the garden.

Walk the access track that runs ahead with the house now to your right. Follow the track, climbing two stiles. After the second, turn left to join a lane. Walk left to pass a house, Woodhaven, and take the signposted footpath on the right. This leads through the garden of the house to a footbridge and stile. Follow the yellow waymarked path through young conifers and then follow the path as it drops downhill to a stile into a pasture.

Continue downhill to a stile to a muddy cart-track, which you cross to another stile by a barn. Head downhill to a stile in the far right corner. Beyond, continue ahead, keeping to the right side of a small stream, where blackthorn is now a cloud of white blossom. Pass through a gate, under which the stream flows, and continue to a small clapper bridge which is edged with mats of golden saxifrage. Stride ahead, following the path as it drops down to come close to the white-topped River Calder. Cross another clapper over Dean Brook and take the stile into Dean Wood. Turn right and climb the stepped path beneath beech.

Stroll the lovely high-level path, with glorious views to the Calder below. Climb the stile out of the wood and turn left to continue through parkland, with the hurrying river to your left. Cross Egg Syke Brook on boulders and Rodger Hey Brook by a footbridge. Beyond the stile strike slightly right towards some cottages on the right. The stile, in the wall to the left of the cottages, gives access to the A680, which you cross, and then turn left to walk across Cock Bridge over the Calder.

Turn right beyond the bridge into a lane leading to a garden centre. Take the footpath, to the left of the entrance, that runs to the right of Cock Wood, which is carpeted with the dark, glossy leaves of bluebells. Stride the wide track. Look right to see the elegant stone Martholme viaduct. Continue to the Whalley Road, which you cross to pass through the splendid gates at the beginning of the track through Read Park. This signposted track passes through parkland. At a branching of tracks, turn left just before Coppy Plantation, a woodland overgrown with rhododendrons. Continue along the track, where curlews fly overhead, until you reach Old Roman Road.

Turn left to cross Read Old Bridge over the Sabden Brook. Here a sparrow hawk tries to fly down a blackbird but this time the prey

Whalley Abbey

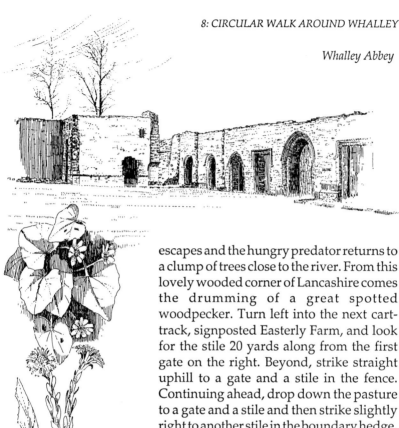

escapes and the hungry predator returns to a clump of trees close to the river. From this lovely wooded corner of Lancashire comes the drumming of a great spotted woodpecker. Turn left into the next cart-track, signposted Easterly Farm, and look for the stile 20 yards along from the first gate on the right. Beyond, strike straight uphill to a gate and a stile in the fence. Continuing ahead, drop down the pasture to a gate and a stile and then strike slightly right to another stile in the boundary hedge. Climb the slope ahead, again bearing slightly right, to the right of the dwellings at Portfield, to a stile to a lane.

Turn right and then right again onto another part of Whalley Road. After 20 yards, where the road swings right, walk ahead, taking the lane signposted 'Cul-de-sac'. Continue ahead, passing the access track to the clubhouse of the golf course. Just beyond, look for the stone stile on the left. Climb steadily right to a stile in the fence ahead. Beyond, strike left, down the slope, and continue over the pasture to a stiled footbridge over a stream which flows below a hedgerow. Look left to see a pretty fall where harts tongue fern and golden saxifrage grow.

Continue ahead, across the corner of the golf course, to a gap stile to the A671. Turn right to walk the few yards to the car park.

9: Circular walk from Hornby

Distance:	7 miles
Time:	3-4 hours
Terrain:	Easy walking all the way
Maps:	OS Landranger 97 Kendal to Morecambe
	or Pathfinder 637 SD 56/57 Burton-in-Kendal and Caton
	628 SD 67/68 Kirkby Lonsdale and Barbon
	650 SD 66/76 High Bentham and Clapham

This walk starts in the pleasing village of Hornby. From its splendid eighteenth century bridge over the River Wenning admire the river and its spectacular weir. Enjoy also the dramatic view of the castle high on its mound, where sheep and lambs graze.

Park in the public car park on the south-west side of the bridge. Cross the bridge and turn left into a gated footpath at its north end and walk beside the river. Birds-eye, wood anemones, celandines and butterbur flower along the path and the soft green leaves of willow are just emerging. Beyond the stile continue along the riverbank, which is now lined with alders laden with catkins. Shelduck and redshanks feed in a flooded pasture and grey wagtails fly upstream in elegant, swooping flight.

At the confluence of the Wenning and the River Lune, turn right to walk upstream of the latter. Skylarks rise from the pastures, carolling melodiously in the mild spring air. A fisherman stands midstream hoping to catch a salmon. Continue along the riverside to a stile that is perched precariously on the edge of the riverbank, giving access to a small wood. Here the steeply sloping floor is carpeted with yellow saxifrage, wood anemones and the green leaves of bluebells. Look for the lovely moschatel, a tiny pale green plant that has five flowers, four facing north, west, south and east and the fifth upwards.

Continue beside the river to a ladder stile that enables you to pass below Loyn Bridge, which has carried traffic to Gressingham since medieval times. On the far side of the bridge, on the right, notice the site of a motte and bailey, a large mound used by the Normans as a defensive position. Those following the circular walk pass the stile on their return, and it is more easily visited then.

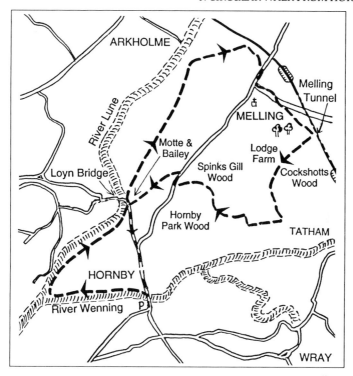

Walk on keeping parallel with the river and alongside an embankment on your right. Continue until the embankment begins to curve right, when you move over left to a concrete tractor bridge over a narrow stream. A heron wings slowly across to the river. Look ahead to the right to see the village of Melling and, behind it, Ingleborough with its top sometimes in cloud and sometimes not. From the bridge walk ahead across a large pasture to a gate in the fence. Continue keeping well clear of a stream, the Old Lune, that emerges from the ground and flows east away from the Lune.

Stride ahead over the pasture, keeping to the right of the stream, aiming for the many-arched viaduct ahead. The path comes to two stiles, close to the water's edge, which you climb. Beyond, follow the track to the right, keeping to the side of the fence. At the waymarked gate pass through and walk the cart-track beyond. Follow the track as it swings right and runs below a railway embankment. Violets flower in the shade of a thorn hedge and the delicate moschatel grows in abundance.

41

Loyn Bridge

Continue along the track and use the clapper bridge to cross a small brook that streams across the way. On reaching the A683, turn right and walk into the village of Melling. Visit the church and view the lovely old houses that line the main road. Turn left between the church and Melling Hall Hotel to walk up the Wennington road. Look through the trees on the right to see another splendid motte.

Continue uphill and turn right and then right again to pass in front of Yew Tree Cottage. Then take a narrow path that runs left between a beech hedge and a paling fence to a stone stile. Beyond, cross a footbridge over a narrow stream. Climb diagonally left to a stile high on the hill from where the air resounds with the calls of curlews. Beyond the stile continue in the same general direction, uphill (right), to a stile in the fence ahead.

Continue on, uphill at first, to a waymarked stile to the left of a small copse. Walk ahead to a reinforced track and turn right to walk to Lodge Farm. To the left stretch the hills of the Forest of Bowland. Bear left to walk to the side of the farm. Pass through the gate and walk ahead, dropping downhill to a stile. Follow the way left, keeping to the right of a depression that soon becomes a steep-sided, tree-lined gill. Primroses line the slopes and a jay flies off, noisily complaining at being disturbed.

At Park House Farm take the second cart-track on the right and walk to a gate. Beyond, continue along the track until it ends at a gate which you pass through. Turn right to walk beside a narrow strip of woodland on your right to a gateless gap into a field. Turn left and continue to a gate in the wall ahead. Beyond, turn right and walk beside the wall on your right either to a difficult stone stile over the wall or, further on, to a gate through it. Pass through the gate and drop downhill to the side of a small conifer plantation and bear left, keeping beside the wall on the right. Larch trees lean over the wall and the spiky leaves are just appearing, the pink roses of a week ago now shaping into small cones. Follow the wall almost to the road and then walk a few yards left to a gate to the A683 which you cross.

Turn right and walk 150 yards to a signposted stiled footpath on your left. The stile gives access to a pasture which you cross diagonally left to a gate into Holme Head Farm. Bear right beyond the gate and continue along a track, below a huge slurry tank, to pass through a silvery gate. Climb the slope and take a similar gate on the left.

Continue ahead to come to the moat of the motte and bailey mentioned earlier. This ancient fortification occupied an ideal defensive position overlooking the Lune. Today it supports magnificent beech trees and Scots pine and its slopes are covered with bluebells. Walk round the moat, which stops at a point where once the River Lune flowed along its side.

Walk on to drop down the slope, past a modern defensive building - a pill-box - to a stile to the lane to Loyn Bridge. Turn left and walk back to Hornby.

Moschatel

10: Circular walk round Sunderland Point

Distance:	4½ miles
Time:	2-3 hours
Terrain:	Easy walking all the way
Map:	OS Pathfinder 659 SD 45/55 Galgate and Dolphinholme

The tiny settlement at Sunderland looks much as it must have done in the eighteenth century when it was developed by a local man, Robert Lawson, as a port for Lancaster's thriving trade with the West Indies. Legend says that the first bales of cotton ever to be landed in Britain arrived there. The lane to the cluster of picturesque dwellings crosses mudflats and saltings. It floods at high tide and then the hamlet can be reached only by footpaths.

This walk, taking you along the shore to the little village and returning over pastures, starts at Middleton Sands. These are approached by Carr Lane, a narrow, winding way that leads from Middleton and ends at the beach. Here you pay 20p to drive onto the sands to park. Walk south along the signposted bridleway as the tide, when high, laps over the fine turf and fills the tidal trenches to your right. Enjoy the far reaching view over the waters of the bay to Knott End and Fleetwood and the glorious expanse of sky with its ever changing pattern of cloud.

From the pastures to your left comes the carolling of skylarks and the evocative call of a courting curlew. Beyond, you can see the Ashton Memorial and Ingleborough. Out on the rapidly disappearing saltings oyster catchers, redshanks, dunlin and ringed plover feed incessantly and large numbers of shelduck move restlessly from shore to pasture. Gorse covered with yellow blossoms grows high on the sand.

Pass on your left the signposted and gated bridleway, The Lane, which turns inland and leads to the centre of the hamlet. Continue on the shore path to a low walled enclosure. Here is buried a negro servant, Sambo, once a sea captain's cabin boy. He came to Sunderland in 1736 and is thought to have died of a fever. He was not allowed to be buried in consecrated ground. On the grave is a plaque inscribed with the following poem written by a Rev James Watson in 1796:

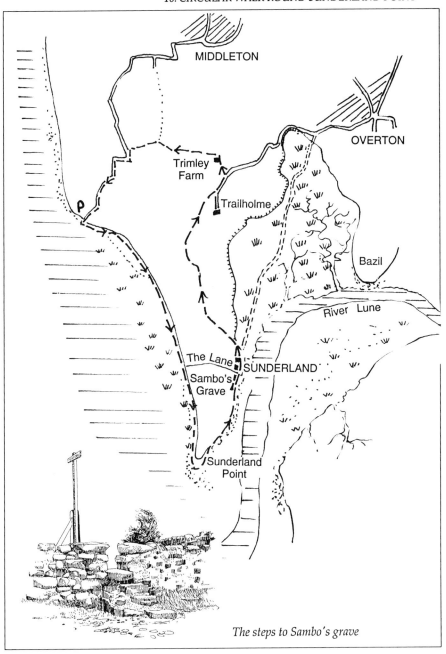

MIDDLETON

OVERTON

Trimley
Farm

Trailholme

Bazil

River Lune

The Lane

SUNDERLAND

Sambo's
Grave

Sunderland
Point

The steps to Sambo's grave

Full sixty years the angry winter's wave,
Has thundering dashed this bleak and barren shore,
Since Sambo's head laid in this lonely grave,
Lies still and ne'er will hear their turmoil more.

Full many a sandbird chirps upon the sod,
And many a moonlight elfin round him trips,
Full many a summer's sunbeam warms the clod
And many a teeming cloud upon him drips.

But still he sleeps - till the awakening sounds,
Of the Archangels trump new life impart,
Then the Great Judge his approbation founds,
Not on man's colour but his worth of heart.

'Sandbirds' still chirp and fresh flowers regularly adorn this quiet corner.

Here you must decide whether to return to walk the bridleway to the hamlet or, if the tide is not too high, to continue along the shore to round Sunderland Point, which is guarded by Plover Scar lighthouse. Among the hawthorn bushes that line the sheltered east bank a sparrowhawk prospects for prey. After you round the point the wide expanse of the Lune estuary stretches to your right and you can just glimpse Glasson Dock, which in time took away all Sunderland's trade.

Dawdle past Sunderland Hall (1683), with its air of a colonial house in the West Indies, and on to walk by a terrace of cottages. One is called Cotton Tree Cottage (1751) after the black poplar that shadows it and each summer is laden with cottony blossom. Then you come to the end of the bridleway, The Lane, and Upsteps Cottage where Sambo died.

Continue along the shore, passing another terrace of pretty cottages and a narrow alley with a tiny cottage built in 1645. At the end of the terrace you can see the posts marking the route of the tide road from Overton to the hamlet. Continue until you reach the white painted ladder stile which you climb to join the footpath to Low Lane. Walk diagonally right to a white painted footbridge, which is hidden by hedgerow foliage, in the far left corner. From now on the footbridges and stiles, all painted white, make the route easy to follow.

Once beyond the hidden footbridge walk ahead to cross two more, keeping beside a ditch on your right. Here on top of a hawthorn bush a reed bunting stammers and stutters its nuptial song. Stride on to the ladder stile in the hedge ahead from where you have a good view of Black Combe. Walk slightly to the right across the next pasture to a high ladder stile, where swallows swoop low over the pasture.

Beyond the stile go along a small embankment with a paved way which leads to a kissing gate. Stroll on to the left of Trailholme Farm to a signposted stile on the right to a concrete access track. Turn left and, in a hundred yards, take the signposted stile on the left to Low Road. Where the track branches, keep to the right fork to pass to the right of all the buildings of Marsh Lea.

Head on to a junction of tracks, climbing the stile on the left in the direction of Carr Lane. Stride ahead to a wooden stile in the fence and then carry on to a stile beside the gate in the far right corner. Go on, with the dyke to your left, to a hidden ladder stile to the right of the left corner. Continue, with the hedge to your left, to the next ladder stile. Beyond, walk a short cart-track to another stile to Carr Lane. Turn left and walk the winding lane to rejoin your car.

The cotton tree, Sunderland Point

47

11: Walk to the Fairy Steps

Distance:	7 miles
Time:	3-4 hours
Terrain:	Easy walking except for the scramble up the Fairy Steps. Walking boots advisable
Maps:	OS Pathfinder 636 SD 37/47 Grange-over-Sands
	637 56/57 Burton-in-Kendal and Caton

The villages of Silverdale, Arnside and Storth border the estuary where the River Kent empties its waters into Morecambe Bay. Silvery limestone hills, with pavement eroded into clints and grykes, erupt from the gentle pastures beyond the villages. Many of these hills are skirted with deciduous woodlands, quaintly named Eaves, Gait Barrows, Cringlebarrow, Middlebarrow and Underlaid. The Fairy Steps are found in the last named.

Park on a deep verge close to the junction of roads at the west end of Yealand Storrs. Pass through a gate to a wide bridlepath through crag-fast ash and yew where cowslips flower. Beyond the next gate continue onwards. Ignore the track that swings left to a broken gate and walk along the grassy track ahead, keeping a wall to your left. Where the track becomes a narrow path through hawthorns, stride on to a metal gate with a squeeze stile beside it.

Strike diagonally right across the pasture to a gap stile half way along a wall. Beyond, continue along the path through a broken wall and, still keeping in a diagonal direction, head for the stile and a nature reserve map in the right-hand corner. Cross the stile, turn right and walk through the glorious beech woodland of New Park. To the left, through the trees, lies Hawes Water, an extensive reed-fringed pool.

At the division of the path, take the right fork and climb through the trees where roe deer roam. At the path end cross the Waterslack road and enter more woodland to the east of Silverdale Moss. Climb a stile out of the woodland, passing into open pasture. Walk on, keeping a wall to the left and limestone outcrops to the right. Where the track is blocked pass through a gap on the right, then continue ahead to a narrow plank bridge over Leighton Beck. Look left here for a good view of Arnside Knott and Arnside Tower. Pass between two copses and continue to a

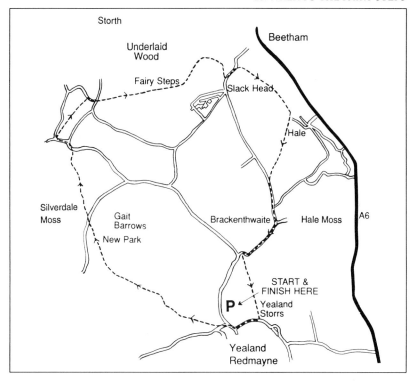

stile beside a gate that gives access to the Arnside road.

Turn left and walk on past Storth Road to take a footpath on the right. Follow the clear path through gorse to a pair of stiles. Take the one on the right and walk across the meadow to join the caravan park access road. Turn right and walk to the gate to Hazelslack. Pause here to view the ruined tower and then turn right. Walk past the farm, cross Storth Road and pass through a gap stile, following the signpost directions to the Fairy Steps.

Once through pastures, with sheep and lambs, pass through a tall gate into Underlaid Wood. Ascend the good path through birch, yew and hazel until the path veers to the left to the base of a limestone wall. Climb the rock steps within a narrow fissure. Continue upwards, following a blue waymark to an even narrower stepped fissure through another high wall of limestone.

Legend has it that fairies used the steps to escape from a witches' cauldron. Enjoy the magnificent views from the top of each rock stairway over the estuary and the viaduct strung out across the water.

"Where roe deer roam . . ."

Walk on through the trees, turning right as directed by the four-armed signpost to Slack Head. Turn left and walk downhill to a footpath on the right. Follow the path along the foot of more woodland until just before Hale. Follow more signposted instructions for Slackhead, leaving the waymarked route at the third left turn. This path ascends through the glorious woodland, over the ridge and then descends close to a caravan site to a narrow country lane. Turn left (south).

Stroll along the quiet lane for half a mile, ignoring two left turns. Just before the third, take the signposted footpath on the left. Follow the indistinct path as it veers slightly to the left. Pass through an open area, then keep to the left of the woodland. Cross left over another open area to a waymarked stile. Beyond, turn right and walk through birch woodland to a stile. Continue ahead to the next stile and walk across the pasture to Yealand Storrs. Turn right and walk through the hamlet to your car.

12: Circular walk around Bleasdale

Distance:	7¹⁄₂ miles
Time:	3-4 hours
Terrain:	Easy walking all the way - but some of the cart-tracks are very muddy after rain and if used by cattle
Map:	OS Pathfinder 668 SD 44/54 Garstang - an essential as few of the rights of way are signposted

Park in a lay-by at Wickins Lane End; the car park opposite the post office and cafe at Bleasdale is reserved for customers. Walk north to pass in front of the post office, once a forge, to cross the River Brock. Turn right into a reinforced track. A noticeboard says 'private road' but the track is a right of way for walkers. It leads through pastures and beside glorious deciduous woodland, with an extensive view to the right of Bleasdale Moors.

Where the track joins a lane continue ahead to pass the village school. A few yards further, in a glorious sylvan setting, stands the parish church of St Eadmer of Admarsh in Bleasdale. Walk on over the cattle-grid and step out along the lane, passing to the right of Vicarage Farm. Cross two cattle-grids and turn right to walk across a pasture, keeping to the left of a fence. Climb the stile, which lies just beyond a solitary beech, and walk to the stile opposite, which gives access to a copse of rowan, beech, oak, birch and Scots pine.

Follow the narrow path to see the Bleasdale Circle. Here in a sunny glade lies a raised barrow, a Bronze Age burial mound once enclosed by a circle of wooden posts, a wooden palisade and a dyke. The remnants of the posts are to be found in a Preston museum; they have been replaced by some rather inappropriate squat concrete pillars.

Continue along the path to a gap on the edge of the wood. Ahead lies Fair Snape Fell and Blindhurst Fell. Look for the dip in the ridge of the latter, called Nick's Chair. Perhaps at a certain time of the year the rising sun shone over the dip onto the wooden circle.

Return to the cattle-grid just before the church, turn right, and walk down a farm-track to cross the cobbled yard in front of Admarsh Barn. Look for the date stone 1720. Stride out along the track to turn right into a narrow lane.

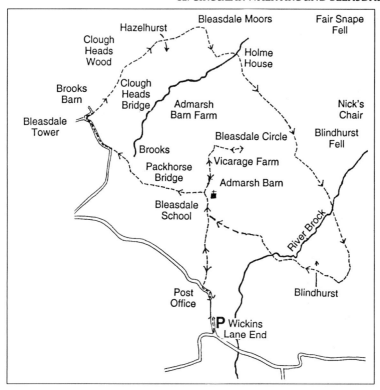

Follow the lane as it drops downhill into a copse and to a sturdy bridge over the River Brock. This was built in the last century by boys from a nearby reformatory. Look upstream to see a perfect packhorse bridge - just wide enough for a horse and with low sides, which would not impede the loads. Continue past Brooks Farm, with its wide cobbled yard, and walk on for half a mile. Turn right in front of Brooks Barn, leaving the lane for a reinforced track. The lane continues to Bleasdale Tower, once the home of William Garnett, a Victorian philanthropist who built and ran the reformatory, but now the home of the Duckworth family.

The next building passed on the right, today estate workers' cottages, was the reformatory, built in 1857. Walk on into Clough Heads Wood and cross the bridge - also built by boys from the reformatory - over the brook of the same name. Pause here and enjoy the tree-lined ravine, through which tumbles the lively stream, and remember the lads who built the bridge over a century ago. Stroll along the track through the

53

deciduous woodland, where a green woodpecker calls.

Pass over a cattle-grid out of the woodland to a magnificent view over the fells. Walk ahead, keeping to the left of Hazelhurst Farm. Beyond the cattle-grid look left to see side-posts, all that remains of some ancient stocks, reminding the walker that this was once a much more populous area and that there were villagers, in addition to the boys from the reformatory, in need of correction!

The way continues past a derelict cottage, under some magnificent beeches and over another cattle-grid. Ignore a waymark pointing onto the fells, and pass through a gate to walk on to Holme House Farm. Beyond, look left to see the zig-zag tracks made by sledges used to bring down peat from the moors.

Walk on along the track to the end of a row of alders edging the stream. Then, where it swings right, turn left and walk to a gate ahead, keeping to the right of a fence. (If you miss this unsignposted left turn you will eventually arrive back at the church.) Beyond the gate walk ahead along the embanked path. Continue along the gated way to pass through the barns of Higher Fair Snape. Walk to the right of two farmhouses (one has a plaque dated 1637), following the track as it swings right, and take a gate on the left, 50 yards beyond the dwellings.

Walk ahead along the gated track. Pass through a gate on the left just before a clump of alders about a stream. Pass through the gate on the right to step across the Brock, where a dipper curtsies on a rock. Another gate gives access to a slope. Continue climbing, crossing three tracks and then keeping to the left of a wall. Head on until you can pass through the wall then strike acute right to Blindhurst. Follow the track as it swings left to pass between the two farmhouses. Drop downhill on a muddy track that soon becomes drier. It continues across a pasture and comes close to a chickenhouse by a gate in a wall. Beyond lies a footbridge over the Brock. Cross and continue ahead to a farm lane which you cross. Carry on over the pasture and through the trees to the track you walked at the start of the walk. Turn left and at the road, turn left to pass Bleasdale post office to return to your car.

Church of St Eadmer of Admarsh in Bleasdale

13: Circular walk from Hurstwood, near Burnley

Distance:	4¹/₂ miles
Time:	2-3 hours
Terrain:	This is a good-weather walk. Easy walking all the way but the path over the moor can be wet after rain and in winter
Map:	OS Pathfinder 681 SD 83/93 Burnley

Deciduous woodland and pastures edge the small village of Hurstwood and over all brood the lonely moors. The hamlet, 5 miles east of Burnley, lies in a hollow close to the River Brun. Two of its charming houses are Hurstwood Hall and Spenser's Cottage.

Park in North West Water's car park, which is reached by a track that leads to the right of the phone box in the centre of the village. Walk to the metalled road to the left (north) of the car park and turn right. Walk the road that runs, for half a mile, south of the coniferous woodland, planted to screen the dam of Hurstwood reservoir from the village. Look for a footpath sign that directs you right, through more conifers, to a green metal gate.

Walk ahead to join and climb a rising track, passing through a hummocky landscape of spoil heaps, evidence of earlier quarrying, now covered by grass. At a post with two waymarks, continue along the left branch, a grassy way bordered with white bedstraw and tormentil. Here skylarks flit about the track. To the right you have a grand view of Cant Clough reservoir (built in 1876), where four adult Canada geese superintend eight large, fluffy goslings and fish leap from the water. Sandpipers call from their pebbly reach of the water's edge.

Continue along the pleasing high-level way, which is also enjoyed by a hare, as it leads into the remote, lonely moorland. Notice the turquoise demoiselle flies that hover over a small pool, surrounded by cotton grass. Stride past more evidence of quarrying to the end of the track. Step out along the continuing footpath that bears north-east towards a red waymarked post.

Follow more waymarked posts and the occasional white painted stones which continue ahead and lead you to a point where you can

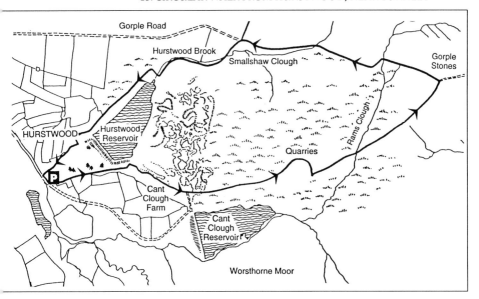

cross Rams Clough, generally keeping your boots dry. Continue on the same north-east diagonal until Gorple Road is reached at Gorple Stones. Turn left on to this reinforced track to return across the moor. Soon the great whaleback of Pendle Hill comes into view. Pass a commemorative seat from where there is a pleasing view down towards Hurstwood.

Walk on towards Hurstwood reservoir, passing a derelict wall on the right. Continue to the next wall on the right and take a wide track on the left. It runs close to Hurstwood Brook. Follow the track as it drops downhill, where more sandpipers call from the stream bed. Cross the footbridge over the stream and continue towards the reservoir. Cross the brook again and climb straight up the slope. Turn left to walk across rough pasture to continue along the edge of a conifer plantation.

Climb a stile into a delightful grassy walled track. Dawdle along the way, which is shaded by beeches, to straddle another stile and continue.

Walk down the steps to a kissing gate to cross a grassy meadow on a path above the reservoir outflow stream. Follow the waymarked post to walk a grassy way between walls to a stile. Walk ahead. To the left a row of stepping stones takes you across the stream to return to the car park. Or you may prefer to walk on into the village and see Hurstwood Hall, built in Elizabethan times (the Hall is not open to the public). Close

to the Hall stands Spenser House, built about 1530. It is believed that the poet Edmund Spenser stayed at the house in 1579. Today part of the building is known as the Gatehouse Tea Cottage. Here you can enjoy a good pot of tea and are made extremely welcome.

Canada geese and sandpipers at Hurstwood Reservoir

14: Circular walk from Arkholme

Distance:	7 miles
Time:	3¹⁄₂ hours
Terrain:	Easy walking all the way. Take care on woodland paths after rain. Walking boots advisable
Map:	OS Pathfinder 637 SD 56/57 Burton-in-Kendal & Caton

To see Lancashire at its best, visit the quiet village of Arkholme and walk through the glorious surrounding countryside. Here rolling pastures support cattle and innumerable sheep, deciduous woodlands resound to the songs of summer migrants and the stately River Lune glides below silvery willows and dark alders.

Park in Arkholme in a turning off the Kirkby Lonsdale road (B6254), close to the village shop. Return to the B road and turn left. Continue along the flower-lined road and take the second signposted footpath on the right, just before the attractive Bainsbeck House. Keep to the right of the outbuildings, where swallows twitter on the wire fence. Bear slightly left across the pasture to the end of a long narrow copse and then continue ahead beside a ditch choked with the thrusting leaves of angelica.

Bear left beyond the waymarked footbridge over a ditch to cross the rolling pasture towards Locka Farm. Follow the waymarks, passing between several dwellings to a narrow lane. Turn left to walk the hedged way, which is lined with flowers. Pass Lower Locka Wood, its lofty beeches towering over a mass of bluebells. At the T-junction, cross the B road and walk right. To your left, through a pleasing tracery of leaves, you can see Storrs Hall, a Tudor Gothic mansion built in 1848 for Francis Pearson, a Kirkby Lonsdale solicitor. It has a striking turreted mock pele tower and an ornate boundary wall.

Just beyond the main gate to the hall pass through a small green gate on your left, signposted 'Gressingham one mile'. Walk the ginnel, below yew, to a stile to pastures. Beyond, head slightly right across the gracious parkland to a stile in the fence. Continue in the same direction across the next pasture, where curious heifers come close, to a signposted stile onto a lane. Turn left to dawdle along another lovely lane which is

59

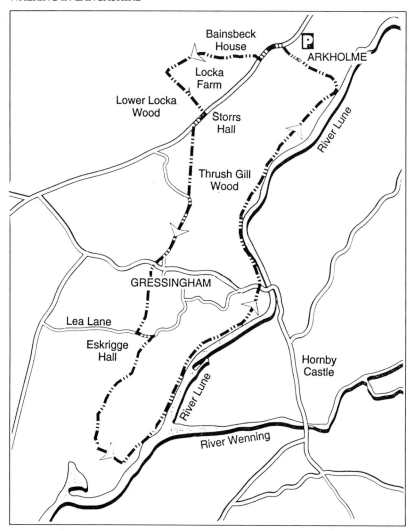

lined with trees from where comes the liquid song of a willow warbler. When the road branches, take the right fork into Gressingham.

Cross the main road and walk down a track into a charming leafy hollow where Gressingham Beck and High Dam Beck meet. The streams are crossed by two white painted footbridges, a pretty fall beneath the second. Stride on to a lane and walk left to pass Far Barn to the signposted footpath on your right. This might be the point to explore the attractive village before continuing on your walk. Visit the pleasing church, St John Evangelist, rebuilt in 1734. Look for the Norman doorway, box pews and a huge Gothic tomb-chest.

Return to the gated track that leads out of the village and take the waymarked stile to the left of two gates. Climb the slope to the next stile in the top right corner and then, with the hedge to your right, head on over a pasture full of noisy green plovers, to a gate to the right of a dwelling. Continue along a short track to Lea Lane. Turn left and climb the narrow leafy lane to pass Eskrigge Hall. At the T-junction enjoy the splendid view of Hornby Castle before swinging right to walk a tarmacked track and then a grassy one.

Where the sunken, grassy way bears sharp left, continue ahead into a pasture - there is no sign of a stile, only an old gate to be climbed. Head on to a difficult gap stile to the right of the junction of two hedges. Beyond, continue with the hedge to your left over a pasture where curlews nest, to a heavy rusty gate, on your left. Pass through and walk on to obtain a magnificent view of the River Lune, a wide silvery ribbon idling through a patchwork of yellow rape and green pastures.

Pass through the gate in the right corner, under an oak. Drop down the slope to a gate at the right end of a fence. Continue, bearing right, beyond the buildings, to another gate to a track densely shadowed with trees. Turn left and walk on to a tall farm gate (easy to miss) on your left which gives access to a huge pasture beside the Lune. Descend the muddy track and bear right, skirting a large pool, where swans nest, to a stile to the side of the placid river. And now begins the magnificent well waymarked upstream riverside walk. Just before the River Wenning empties its waters into the Lune a fly-fisherman casts for salmon. The way continues through shady deciduous woodland, the haunt of a woodpecker and a jay, and continues over pasture to the medieval Loyn Bridge.

As you walk look for a graceful sandpiper, uttering its cheery note as it skims the water. Watch out also for the vivid petrol-blue flash of a kingfisher and for a merganser carrying two of her brood of eight on her folded wings. Oyster catchers abound and these you cannot fail to see, but the shy redshank with its haunting trilling is more difficult to spot.

Climb the step stile to the left of the bridge, cross the road, and take the continuing waymarked path beside the river to pass through Thrush Gill wood. Beyond, the stiled path moves away from the river and then comes back to its side. Here swifts, swallows and house martins hunt for flies in the warm afternoon sun. Continue to the end

Storrs Hall and jay

of the path and follow the signpost to Arkholme. Climb the hill and go along the pretty street, which is lined with houses bearing seventeenth and eighteenth century date plaques, to rejoin your car.

15: Circular walk from Dolphinholme via Abbeystead Reservoir

Distance:	6¹/₂ miles
Time:	3-4 hours
Terrain:	Easy walking except for the climb down to Long Bridge half a mile from Swainshead Hall
Map:	OS Pathfinder 659 45/55 Galgate and Dolphinholme

It is good to have a purpose for a walk. Enjoying the gentle pastures and flower-carpeted deciduous woodland about the River Wyre is purpose enough, but visiting the lake-like Abbeystead reservoir, with its abundant bird life, and the well designed weir with its teeming fish gives an added pleasure.

Park by the church of St Mark's, Dolphinholme. Walk north-east along the road in the direction of the school and take the right turn just before the wall of the school. At the end of the short road, swing left to descend the steep footpath to Lower Dolphinholme and the River Wyre. Turn right to cross the bridge over the surging water, where a pair of dippers dive into the rapids after prey. Walk uphill to take a stiled footpath on the right, signposted Wagon Road.

Climb the path between conifers to a metal stile to open pasture. Look left to see a derelict double chimney where once smoke issued, piped from a worsted mill in the valley. Bear slightly left to the stile ahead, beneath a row of Scots pine and birch. Beyond, walk the path through the trees where a willow warbler sings, its thin, pointed beak opening and closing rapidly to allow the sound to fill the air. Take the stile on the left and strike diagonally right to a cedarwood footbridge which gives access to Wagon Road.

Take the stile opposite and walk ahead, where sheep feed their lambs. Climb the stile beside a ditch, turn right and pass through the gap stile to Tinker's Lane. Turn left. Stride along the quiet lane, bordered with oak and willow, beneath which flower violets and wood sorrel. Watch out for the narrow Street Brook, beyond which you turn left to take a stile into more pasture. Cross diagonally right, passing through two gates, and continue along a track to Stonehead Farm. Pass through

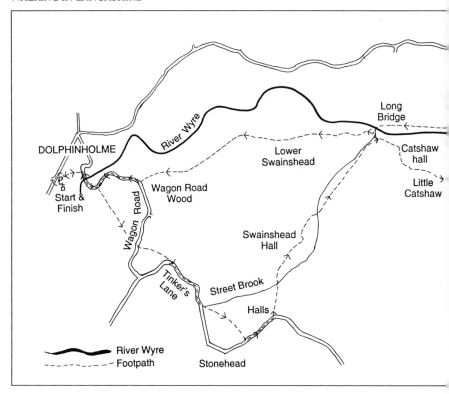

two obvious gaps in a walled area, a gate and the farmyard to Long Lane. Turn left and step out to Halls. Beyond, where the road turns sharp right, climb the waymarked stile on the left.

Follow the yellow arrows on the fence, on the left, to a gate. Beyond, cross Street Brook by a small plank footbridge. Here a long-legged hare races across the spring pastures. Follow the path, bearing right to a ladder stile to the right of Swainshead Hall. Walk across a small walled area to the next stile and turn left beyond. Pass in front of some horse stabling and take a gate to the right of the farm road.

Walk downhill over pasture, diagonally right, to a gate on the right, beyond the Street Brook. Walk ahead for nearly half a mile, keeping the fence to the left. Overhead, meadow pipits soar upwards, five or six at a time, singing ecstatically. Look for a stile in the far left corner which gives access to a steep slope. The way lies downhill, passing between newly planted trees to the side of the River Wyre. Do not cross the Long Bridge over the river, but follow a clear path bearing slightly to the right

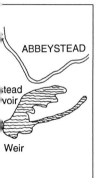

through tall oaks. A cloud of bluebells perfume the air. The path leads to a wooden footbridge across Hall Gill Beck. Climb the steep slope to the stile and continue up a wide track to a gate.

Beyond, turn right and walk over the pasture to Catshaw Hall which has a stone plaque dated 1678. Follow the farm road to the left and take the left branch to Little Catshaw (1763). Pass through two gates and walk ahead along a wide cart-track. Just before the next gate, turn left and walk across the pasture to pass through a gate. Drop downhill to the side of the River Wyre. Cross Cam Brook on the right by a footbridge and then take the iron bridge over the hurrying river. To the right towers the dam of Abbeystead reservoir, softened and shadowed by the lovely deciduous woodland. Notice the splendid weir to the right.

Turn right and cross the stepped fish-pass to climb the steps to the walkway of the dam. Ahead lies the pleasing expanse of tree-lined water - Abbeystead reservoir, named after an earlier abbey established by the monks of Furness Abbey.

Return to the iron bridge but do not cross. Pass through a stepped stile in the wall and follow the waymarked footpath that keeps parallel to the river, until you reach Long Bridge. Cross and bear right, climbing uphill through the trees to a stile to pasture. Bear right, keeping below Lower Swainshead. Cross the gutter by a footbridge and continue ahead to join a cart-track. Follow this until reaching Wagon Road. Turn right and walk downhill to the bridge over the Wyre at Dolphinholme. Climb the footbridge on the left, taken earlier, to return to your car.

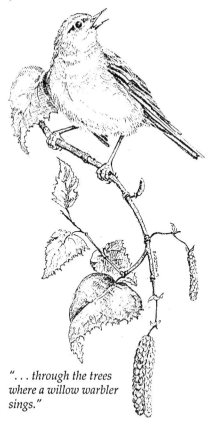

"... through the trees where a willow warbler sings."

16: Circular walk to Darwen Hill and Roddlesworth Reservoirs

Distance:	6¹/₂ miles
Time:	3-4 hours
Terrain:	Easy walking for most of the way. Short climb to Darwen Tower and from the reservoir to the car park
Map:	OS Landranger 103 Blackburn, Burnley and surrounding area

On this pleasing walk you climb to the top of the Jubilee Tower on Darwen Hill; you pass two secluded reservoirs; you descend to the 'hollow of Toca', Tockholes; you continue past farmhouses built in the seventeenth century and you return through lush spring woodland.

Park at the Roddlesworth Information Centre next to the Royal Arms at the top of the hill close to the hamlet of Ryal Fold. Return to the road and turn left. Turn left again into Hollinshead Terrace, following a two-armed signpost. This row of cottages was built for people who worked at the one-time Tockholes cotton mill. Turn right immediately before the cottages, to pass through an awkward kissing gate. Ahead, steadily climbing, stretches a wide reinforced track, perhaps one of the old coach roads. As you ascend look left for a good view of, first, Earnsdale reservoir in its valley and, then, Sunnyhurst Hey, set in hilly pastures. Ahead stands Jubilee Tower on Beacon Hill.

Pass through the stile beside the gate and walk the railed track through mixed woodland. Continue as it swings left with a view of the reservoir ahead. Before the next gate take the narrower track on the right that swings back above the track just walked. Climb steadily upwards and follow the track as it swings left at the top of the slope. Continue to a stile onto heather-clad moorland, where grouse call and skylarks rise, carolling. Turn left to walk a good track and at a junction take the right branch to come to the foot of the tower.

It was erected in 1898 to commemorate the diamond jubilee of Queen Victoria. Inside, it has wide shallow steps leading to an outside walled parapet with glorious views over rural Lancashire. More steps

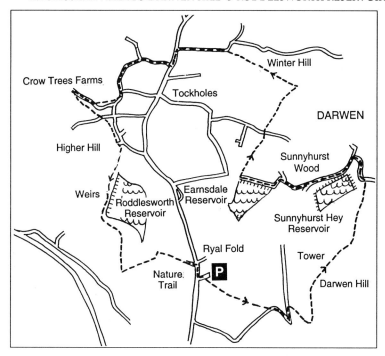

lead to a door that gives access to another parapet and even more extensive views.

On leaving the tower, continue in the same direction as taken before - north-east - following the track downhill, with Sunnyhurst Hey reservoir to the left. Pass through a gate and continue to the metalled road. Turn left and walk past Sunnyhurst Wood on the right, the road soon becoming a track. Stride on past the water board cottage, built in 1898. At the junction of tracks take the right fork and follow it as it swings right into quiet pastures where sheep graze. Continue along the dam of Earnsdale reservoir from where you can see a pair of golden-eye ducks, startlingly black and white, idling on the silvery water, with heads held characteristically high.

Cross the cattle-grid and ascend the concrete track. Look for the wind pump on the left and then continue to Berry's Tenement Farm. At the entrance to the farmyard, on the left, stands a millstone, with the words 'In memory of Abella wife of Duxbury' inscribed upon it. Turn left by the millstone and pass through a gate. Turn right beyond the barn, keeping beside the wall on your right, to a stile by a gate.

Jubilee Tower, Toches Stone and Higher Hill farm

Continue straight ahead along a wide track to a point half way across the golf course. Just beyond a wooden shelter, in which stands a commemorative seat, turn left and walk uphill, along another track, to a gate in a wall. Beyond, turn right and stride out, keeping the wall to the right. Ignore the small footpath signs into the settlement at Winter Hill and walk on to pass through two stiles very close together. Stride ahead across a pasture to the start of an old track, which continues onwards. Notice on your right - but do not pass through - an enormous wrought iron gate with an old stone gap stile beside it.

Stride along the very wet grassy track to a gate to Coal Pit Lane, which you walk to the road. Turn left and take the next right turn, Rock Lane, beyond the Rock public house. Just before St Stephen's church and school, notice, on the right, the stone used as a lintel of a doorway and inscribed 1692. A few yards beyond look for a well set below a Norman-shaped arch.

Continue to the church, which has an arched porch, all that remains of an earlier one built in about 1833. The porch gives entrance to a modern church (1965) beyond. To the left of the arch is the Toches stone. The legend on the lower part, a cheese press, tells that the upright stone is supposed to be a remnant of a preaching cross, possibly dating from the year 684. Below this is the ancient Toches stone, from which the parish takes its name. As you leave the churchyard, by the lower gate, look left to see the school, built in 1834 with a stone open-air pulpit in front.

Turn right to walk down the lane. Pass Lodge Farm and take the stile on the right. Strike across the pasture, behind the chapel to another stile. Continue over the next pasture to a stone stile to walk through a farmyard to a lane. Turn right and detour to see two seventeenth century farmhouses, Higher and Lower Crow Trees, which still retain some mullioned windows.

Walk back past the higher farmhouse and take the stone steps on the right that lead to a stile. Beyond, walk diagonally left to a stile in the corner and follow the fenced track to another lane. Here is the seventeenth century Lower Hill Manor Farm, now converted to four cottages. Take the stile opposite and walk uphill, following the wall to Higher Hill Farm, another magnificent house built in 1612.

Look for the footpath sign and stile on the access track to the farm. Beyond the stile follow the wall on the right to the next signpost. Pause by the wall to see a medieval latrine, high on the south side of the house. Descend to a kissing gate, which leads into woodland. Turn left and at the junction take the right branch to walk along the dam of one of the Roddlesworth reservoirs. Turn left at the end of the dam and stroll through the glorious woodland. Keep to the right branch until you reach a brook which you cross by a bridge. Continue left along the brook towards the reservoir again and then take a right turn by the nature trail sign. Climb through the woodland until you reach the Royal Arms and the car park.

17: Circular walk from Dunsop Bridge

Distance:	10 miles
Time:	5 hours
Terrain:	Nothing too arduous. Several parts of the walk can be very muddy or boggy after rain
Map:	OS Pathfinder 660 SD 65/75 Slaidburn and Forest of Bowland

This is a great walk for those who like quiet pastures, the haunt of ground nesting birds, and lonely moors where grouse call from acres of glorious heather. It should be done in good weather, not after heavy rain or when the tops are misty.

Park at Dunsop Bridge, the small village that lies at the foot of the Forest of Bowland. Turn right as you leave the car park to pass the garage, once a blacksmith's forge and the hub of the village. Continue past the post office to cross Dunsop Bridge over the River Dunsop. Climb the hill to turn right before the war memorial to walk the signposted bridleway. Enjoy the dramatic view of the fells ahead. Continue past the Forestry Commission buildings and then Closes Barn. Walk on to cross the wooden bridge over the Dunsop and turn right to walk beside the lively, alder-lined river.

A hundred yards along take the path on the left. It climbs steeply through ash trees, and a wonderful carpet of bluebells, to a stile in the wall into a pasture. Bear slightly left and, following the line of overhead cables, climb the slope to join a farm-track. Turn left and walk past the two solitary dwellings at Beatrix which command a good view of the pastures and slopes around. It is difficult to imagine that this was once a thriving community that held its own market.

Where you reach two gates, pass through the one on the left. Turn sharp left to walk the raised ground above the farm until you reach the fence. Turn right to walk up the pasture and pass through the gate in the fence. Follow the cart-track and then bear right to cross the pasture on a right diagonal to a stile. Beyond, keeping the ditch to the left, walk ahead to a copse. Drop down the steepish slope of Oxenhurst Clough to cross a stream. Walk ahead to a small rickety gate in the left-hand

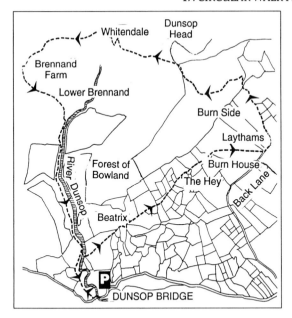

corner of the fence, into young larch where a willow warbler fills the air with its song.

Continue up a tormentil-clad slope on a narrow path with a ditch to the right and a deep gill to the left. Climb the fence into a pasture and continue ahead, with the ditch to the right. Climb the next fence, where there was once a stile, now lying broken on the ground. Continue ahead to a tar-macked cart-track where you bear left to pass The Hey and then the seventeenth century Burn House.

Pass through the gate and then, 50 yards along, leave the track and strike right across a huge pasture to a stone stile in the boundary wall. Beyond, continue in the same direction to pass to the left of an old air-raid shelter to cross a farm-track. Continue in the same right diagonal to a stile in the fence. Beyond, in the same direction, continue across a pasture where green plovers nest. In a scrape of dead grass lie four oval-shaped pale brown eggs speckled with dark brown blotches. Walk to a gate opposite three cottages, named Laythams, and turn left to walk Back Lane where gypsywort and water avens grow.

Turn left at the signposted lane and continue to pass through the gate to the right of Burn Side. Follow the waymarks to reach the raised path that climbs steadily to the fell gate. Follow the path, which climbs steeply right and, just beyond a clump of straggly pine and sycamore, continue where it swings sharp left. Walk the airy grassy way that climbs steadily to the top of Burn Fell. When the wall comes into sight, bear right across a wet area and continue right to the gate, in the wall, at Dunsop Head.

Follow the waymarked path through heather and bilberry, from

Grouse butt on shooters' path above the Whitendale River

where grouse call, and continue down the zig-zagging shooters' path to Whitendale, which nestles in a moorland hollow on the Whitendale River. Cross the gated footbridge, climb the steep slope ahead and follow the waymarked track to a gate. Follow the waymarks to a ladder stile to the left of a small tarn. Walk ahead, where curlews and oyster catchers fly overhead. Continue past spoil heaps from ancient mineworkings; lead and silver were wrested from the fells. Beyond the gate turn left and then right where the stiled track swings down to Brennand Farm - it too set in a hollow in the fells.

Cross Brennand River and beyond keep to the left of the house. Look for the old shooters' wagon that was once drawn by horse to carry refreshments onto the fell. Continue on a tarmacked lane to cross the river again and walk on past Lower Brennand to the T-junction. Continue downhill, taking the branch to the right. From now on the metalled road is edged with conifers to the left. At Foot Holme cross the river where the Whitendale and Brennand rivers join to become the Dunsop. Pass water board buildings. Stride on now, with the Dunsop on the left and conifers on both sides. From the trees comes the call of a cuckoo. Continue until you reach Dunsop. Cross the bridge to regain your car.

18: Circular walk from Whitewell via Stakes and Doeford Bridge

Distance:	7½ miles
Time:	4 hours
Terrain:	Easy walking all the way, except for two muddy lanes. Do not cross the hipping stones at Stakes unless all are fully exposed. Do not expect to cross the River Hodder at Whitewell unless the gravel bed is exposed
Map:	OS Pathfinder 669 SD 64/74 Clitheroe and Chipping. Use a map for this walk because very few of the footpaths are signposted

The Trough of Bowland is a trough of tranquillity. High fells surround green pastures through which flows the stately River Hodder. Through this quiet peacefulness this walk passes, taking in pastures, woodland, riverside, winding lanes and farmhouses, the latter retaining architectural features of days gone by.

Park in the car park below St Michael's Church at Whitewell. Walk back to the road, passing the Whitewell Hotel on the left. Cross the road and climb uphill, in the direction of Cow Ark, keeping to the left of the white-painted village hall. A few steps along the road bring you to a footpath sign on the right. Climb stone steps to enter a pasture and walk ahead to a small gateway. Beyond, bear to the right of a house to join a track.

Follow the track right. Look right for an extensive view along the lovely trough, with wooded slopes about green fields, and to the graceful two-arched Burnholme Bridge. Pass through the left of two gates. Leave the track and turn right, following the wall on the right, to continue ahead to an iron kissing gate. From here onwards the dominant sound of the walk is the trilling song and the long, liquid, bubbling call of innumerable curlews.

As you continue keep close to a fence on the right to walk to the next stile. Below, hidden in the wooded valley bottom, flows the River Hodder. Three hares stand on their back legs and box and then, when disturbed, lope off in different directions over the slopes. Pass through

73

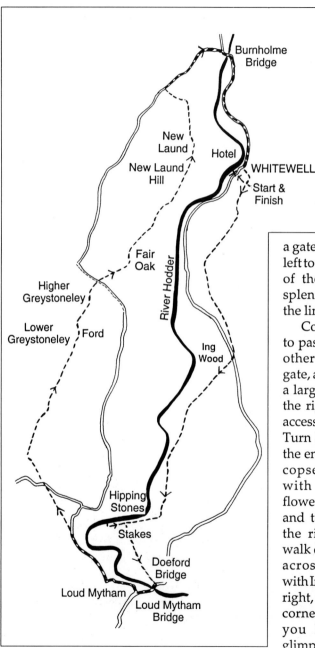

a gate and then look left to the cam stones of the wall to see splendid fossils in the limestone.

Continue ahead to pass through another iron kissing gate, and walk on to a large iron gate on the right that gives access to the road. Turn left to walk to the end of the small copse, spangled with the yellow flowers of coltsfoot, and take a stile on the right. Beyond, walk diagonally left across a pasture, with Ing Wood to the right, to a stile in the corner. From here you have a first glimpse of the River

Hodder. Continue along a faint grassy trackway, either above or below a limestone outcrop, to ford a tributary stream. Walk ahead to cross a plank over a ditch to a stile over a fence and continue ahead keeping parallel to the lovely river, which is edged with alders. Pause here to watch dippers, redshanks and oyster catchers busy with their nuptials.

Climb the fence to cross another ditch on a small plank. On the edge of the river stands a wooden structure, sheltering a seat which must be ideal for bird watching. Just beyond stand some huge gnarled elms. Cross a narrow ditch and climb up the slope to pass through a gate to a farm lane.

Turn right and walk to Stakes Farm, which stands solidly beside the river. It belongs to the Duchy of Lancaster. Over a doorway of this very pleasing, much mullioned late-Stuart farmhouse is a Latin inscription about the unpredictability of life. Across the river stretches a row of hipping stones (stepping-stones), to be used only when the river is low. This is the haunt of kingfishers, grey wagtails, herons and dippers.

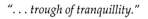

". . . trough of tranquillity."

75

Return along the lane and pass through two farm gates on the right in front of a barn. Turn left and climb the slope to a gate ahead. Walk ahead, keeping to the left of the hedge. Pass through a gate on the left and walk diagonally left across the pasture to drop down to a squeeze stile to the road. Turn right to cross the double-arched Doeford Bridge and continue along the road. Turn right, onto a lane signposted Little Bowland, to cross Loud Mytham Bridge over the River Loud. Pass Loud Mytham, a charming mullioned seventeenth century farmhouse, to walk the narrow lane. Ignore a footpath sign on the left at a point where the lane begins to make a large curve to the right and continue to a stile (not signposted), also on the left, into a pasture, opposite woodland. Walk ahead to the far left corner to a stile to the road, with a fine view of the fells. Cross, and walk up the long farm-track to newly built Lower Greystoneley.

Beyond the farm, walk downhill through the trees where flower violets, primroses, wild strawberry, wood anemones and wood sorrel. Cross a wooden bridge, upstream of a ford, over a narrow stream. Stride uphill along the track to pass Higher Greystoneley (1873). Just beyond, take a stile on the right to cross a pasture to a stile to the road. Cross to the stile opposite and walk ahead over another and then ahead to a farm lane. Turn left and pass Fair Oak Farm. Turn right to walk an excessively muddy farm-track out into pastures. Continue, keeping the fence to the left to cross a stile. Walk on beside the stone wall on your left until you reach a ladder stile.

Cross this and bear right to walk the upper grassy trackway over New Laund Hill. To the right lie the deciduous wooded steep slopes of Whitewell Gorge. Look back from here for a splendid view of the River Hodder. Pass through the gate in the electrified fence and drop down the steepish slope to New Laund Farm. Here turn left to walk the farm-track to join the road. Turn right and continue to Burnholme Bridge. Cross, and walk the mile to Whitewell.

19: Circular walk from Nether Burrow

Distance:	6½ miles
Time:	3-4 hours
Terrain:	Easy walking all the way. Some high stiles to be climbed
Map:	OS Pathfinder 628 SD 67/68 Kirkby Lonsdale and Barbon

In July parent birds busily deal with persistently demanding young. Fields are lush with flowering grasses, buttercups and clover. Dog daises turn their faces to the sun and sorrel adds a rich redness to the meadows. Overhead, swallows and house martins hawk flies in the afternoon sun. It is just right for a walk through a quiet corner of Lancashire, where for nearly all the time you are far from the noise and bustle of roads and towns.

Park in the car park of the Highwayman Inn, Nether Burrow, 2½ miles south of Kirkby Lonsdale. The landlord welcomes walkers and likes them to use the space to the south of the inn. The inn was once a hunting lodge for the Fenwick family who lived at Burrow Hall. Notice the fine coat-of-arms over the entrance. The stables for the lodge, now a private house, stand opposite and next to them is the old laundry, similarly converted.

Walk north through the tiny village, along the A683 to the two-arched Burrow Bridge over the Leck Beck. It was constructed in 1735. Turn right just before the bridge and descend the signposted wooden steps to the bank of the river. Climb the stile ahead and walk upstream beside the hurrying water, dappled with sunlight, passing through alders, oaks and sycamores. The path moves diagonally right out into the long pasture, coming beside a mixed plantation from where a green woodpecker calls.

Take the gate to the far right of Parkside Farm. Follow the track as it swings left and continue between outbuildings. Take the gate to the left of a garage that gives access to a track where mistle thrushes probe. Continue onwards, with a superb view of Ingleborough ahead of you, to a gate that lies behind a large oak. Beyond lies Woodman Lane, along which you walk right. The lane is hedged with blackthorn, hawthorn, bird cherry, rowan, elder, sycamore and honeysuckle - the latter laden

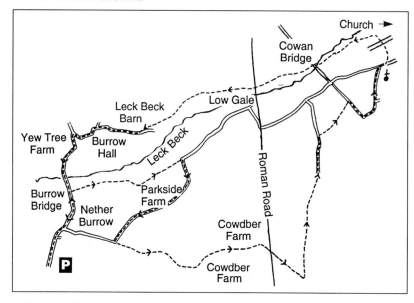

with sweetly scented blossoms.

At the sharp bend in the lane, where it swings right, turn left to walk a wide track with a little stream running beside it. Continue ahead, walking close to Cowdber Wood, where a blackcap sings its short mellow song. Stride past Cowdber Farm and then walk through two gates and continue over a pasture to a gate in the left corner. Just beyond the gate look for the grassy embankment, running north-west. This is the foundation of a Roman road and would have been used by soldiers on their way to the fort sited on a promontory between Leck Beck and the River Lune.

Cross the embankment and bear right to a gate in the wall beyond a small stream. Pass through the gate and continue in the same diagonal to a stile over a wire fence. Step out in the same way to another stile over another wire fence. Continue right to a gate. Beyond, turn left and climb uphill to a gate in the hedge. Continue uphill to pass through a small gate into a pasture where curlews protect their second broods.

Stride on, keeping to the right of the hedge to climb the stone stile in the boundary wall ahead. Continue in the same direction to climb the next stile. Walk diagonally right to a gate that gives access to a wide walled track, just beyond a barn on your right. The grassy track is a joy to walk and then for a very short distance becomes overgrown with thorn bushes. Where you reach the end of this rough part look for a stone stile, with a very high first step, in the wall on the right under a large oak.

Walk ahead from the stile, with the hedge to your left. Continue in the same direction, climbing a stile in each of three boundary walls, enclosing pastures. Here green plovers wheel and dive when you come too close to their nests. Stride ahead to a signposted gap stile to the A65, which you cross. Turn right and take the first left turn to walk the narrow hedged lane, which leads to the village of Leck. Turn right at the

Nether Burrow

crossroads and walk ahead. Look right to see the pleasing church of St Peter. After a fire, the church was rebuilt in 1912 to the original design of Paley and Austin (1878-9).

Just before the right turn to the church, take the gap stile in the wall on the left. Walk ahead, keeping to the right of a barn. Continue to a stile to a narrow track to the left of a cottage. Walk the grassy track to the road which you cross to a gap stile. Stride ahead to come to the side of Leck Beck. Turn left and dawdle through the lovely elm and alder woodland that edges the river. Dippers and grey wagtails fly upstream as they are disturbed from tending their broods.

As you near the viaduct over the river take the stile through a wall ahead and walk to a gap stile onto the A65. Cross to pass through another gap stile and turn right to walk over the bridge. Turn left to descend a grassy slope to the bank of the Leck. A grassy way through thorn bushes leads you downstream to join a metalled track, along which you continue. Pass two footbridges and then, before the cattle-grid, take a stile on your right. Turn left and walk to the right of Low Gale. Beyond the broken stile walk to the far right corner to a stile over the fence to a stone footbridge across a small stream which was bordered with primroses in the spring.

Climb the slope and continue parallel with the Leck. A heron rises from a ditch and flies off slowly and a pair of oyster catchers pipe and scold when disturbed. Drop down the slope to a stile over the wall to the left of a tiny brook. Directly ahead stands the imposing Burrow Hall. Continue ahead and just before joining a farm-track look left to see an unusual stile. Pass through the gate by Leck Beck Barn and walk on to the next gate. Beyond, walk through a small settlement to the A683. Turn left and pass Yew Tree Farm to stroll to Burrow Bridge. Continue along the road to rejoin your car.

20: Circular walk from Conder Green Picnic Site

Distance:	6 miles
Time:	3-4 hours
Terrain:	Easy walking all the way
Map:	OS Pathfinder 659 SD 45/55 Galgate & Dolphinhome

This walk takes you along the Lancashire Coastal Way from Conder Green to Glasson basin and dock. It continues beside the quiet waters of the Glasson branch of the canal and returns you over pastures where green plovers and meadow pipits fill the air with their evocative calls.

Park in the car park on the site of the old Conder Green Station. To reach this turn off the Lancaster to Cockerham road (A588) by the Stork Hotel and continue west to the end of the minor road. Leave the car park, walking south-west along the Lancashire Coastal Way, which was opened in September 1991. The way follows the route of the Lancaster-Glasson Dock railway, a branch line of the former London and North Western Railway, which opened in 1883. Its rails were removed in 1962.

Cross the bridge over the River Conder and enjoy the extensive views over the estuary of the River Lune to Bazil Point and Sunderland. The track is lined with blackberry in flower, tufted vetch, rest harrow, hop trefoil, St John's wort, agrimony, tom thumb, silver weed and yarrow. Curlews call from the estuary and fly overhead.

On reaching a long stretch of grass beside the estuary continue ahead to pass the bowling green. To the right sea thrift colours the sea wall and, beyond, spartina grass binds the mud. Turn left as directed by the signpost and then right at the B5290. Take the left turn, opposite the Victoria Inn, to stand on the swing bridge, which is flanked by lock gates and footbridges. To the north lies the dock, where several sea-going vessels unload their cargo and others take on large containers. To the south of the bridge many colourful boats are moored in the large canal basin now used as a marina.

Glasson Dock was developed when the River Lune silted up in the 1780s and ships were unable to reach St George's Quay, Lancaster.

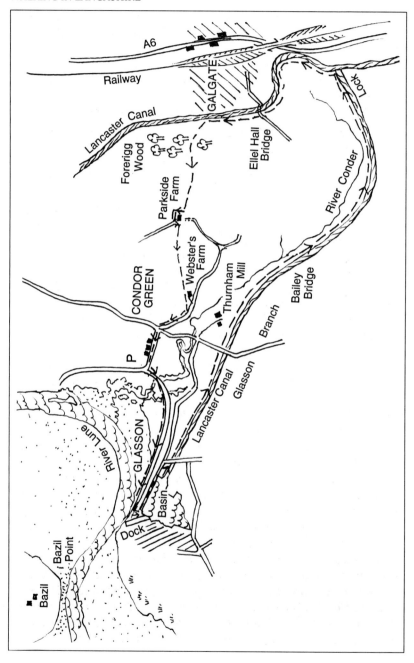

Ships took coal to Cornwall, bringing back china clay. Timber, wood pulp and iron ore all arrived at the dock. The Glasson branch of the canal was opened in 1826.

Return from the bridge and take the path on the right just beyond a cafe. This takes you beside the basin. Follow the signpost directions to walk the glorious towpath. To your left a small gate gives access to Christ Church, with its fine bell tower, built 14 years after the canal. Immediately after the church you pass under Brows Bridge, a skew bridge, number 8. Here a cuckoo sits on an overhead wire.

Continue along the waterway, which is lined with meadow sweet, kidney vetch, comfrey and marsh woundwort. A family of coots swim close to the bank and oyster catchers call from the meadows close by. Soon the water's edge is lined with reeds and many are 6 feet high, obscuring the water beyond. Pass below the railed Brick Kiln Bridge, number 7, and stride on to walk below Thurnham Bridge, number 6. Beyond stands Thurnham Mill, once a water-powered cornmill. Today it is a hotel and restaurant with an attractive canalside tavern. Once a channel of water from the River Conder led to the mill to drive its machinery. Now the channel is dry but some of the old machinery, still in place, has been painted and forms part of the decor of the tavern.

By the old mill is the first of a flight of six locks before the mainline canal. Each lock has a small weir at the side to take off excess water and a footbridge giving access to the opposite bank. Continue beside the cut and its locks, passing below bridges 5, 4, 3 and 2 to come to the cobbled Junction Bridge, number 1, a turnover bridge. This type of bridge enabled a boat to continue without the horse being disconnected.

Follow the towpath left to walk beside the mainline waterway, passing the lock-keeper's cottage. Just before bridge 86 is the Galgate marina. The towpath is shadowed by willow and elder. Head on, beneath the bridge, to come to the Conder aqueduct, bridge 87. Lean over to see the River Conder hurrying beneath the low arch. Look for the buttresses and curving walls. Then you pass below Ellel Hall Bridge, number 88. Press on until you are opposite the last dwelling in Galgate and take the stile in the hedge on your left.

Beyond, strike diagonally right across the meadow to climb a stile and continue beside Forerigg Wood, now on your left. Enter the wood by a metal stile and walk the narrow path through the trees to leave by a similar stile. Head across the pasture, to a metal stile in the left corner. Beyond, follow the field boundary, with a hedge to your right, to a stile beside a gate, on your right. Continue in the same general direction along a track to Parkside Farm. Pass through the farm buildings and the yard to a stone-stepped stile in the wall ahead.

Continue ahead, with the boundary on your right, to a metal ladder stile. Beyond, stride on with the hedge to your right to the side of Crow Wood. Here the right of way takes you over a stile and then a stiled stone slab footbridge and a small gate, all in a few yards. Turn left to continue walking, west, with the boundary to your left to a gate. Beyond head on to pass the back of Webster's Farm to a tall ladder stile onto Galgate road, where you turn right.

Walk the lane to join the A588. Turn left and then right in front of the Stork Inn to walk the quiet minor road to rejoin your car.

Coot and moorhen at bridge 6 on Glasson Branch

21: Circular walk from Wycoller

Distance:	6 miles
Time:	3-4 hours
Terrain:	Easy walking all the way
Map:	OS Pathfinder 681 SD 83/93 Burnley

Wic-air is the Anglo-Saxon name for Wycoller and means the dairy farm among the alders, at one time the predominant tree in the area. Then the land was cleared and the trees cut down. Today a young plantation of alders is thriving on the slopes above the little settlement.

Park in the car park at the end of Trawden Road above the village of Wycoller and leave by the footpath, at the end. The way, a third of a mile, runs beside the narrow lane into the hamlet. Enjoy this pleasing corner with its thirteenth century twin-arched packhorse bridge and, further upstream, its clapper bridge. This is formed of two slabs supported by stone piers, and worn to a trough shape by the clogs of generations of weavers, taking their cloth to the tenterfield above the ruins of Wycoller Hall. Look up on the slope above the hall to see the thirteenth century vaccary walls, slabs of stone used as boundaries to enclose cattle.

It is difficult to believe that 350 people lived in the settlement in 1820. The villagers were handloom weavers. With the development of the powerloom they had to move away to find jobs. The Bronte sisters

Packhorse bridge, Wycoller

85

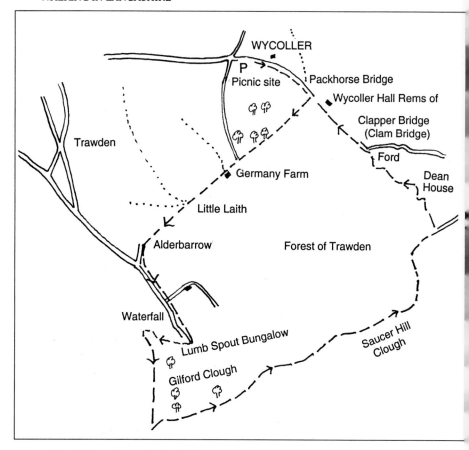

visited Wycoller and the hall may have been the original of the Ferndean Manor in *Jane Eyre*. By 1950 the hamlet was almost deserted.

What a glorious place to start a walk! Continue along the metalled road and bear right following the sign 'No through road, public footpath'. Look for the waymarked path on the right. Climb the stepped way through lush vegetation to a stile, to continue between a wall on your right and woodland on the left. Follow the good path through alders to a waymarked sturdy stone stile with Raven's Rock Farm away to the left. Pause to take in the magnificent view of east Lancashire, with Pendle Hill towering over all.

Stride on the stiled way to pass Germany Farm. Pass in front of Little Laith and take the gated stile to the left of a metalled gate. Beyond, pass through the gate immediately on your left. Continue down the pasture,

Clapper bridge, Wycoller

with the wall away to your right, towards Alderbarrow with its two-armed Pendle Way signpost, complete with witches on broomsticks. Join the farm's access track and walk to a narrow lane. Turn left.

Continue to where the lane swings sharp left to walk ahead along the Pendle Way. Keep to the left of the farm, remaining on the good gated track. Drop down the slope to a tractor bridge over a hurrying beck. Turn right, following the indistinct sign for the waterfall, Lumb Spout. Continue along the high ground above the stream to see the splendid single white spout tumbling elegantly into a dark brown pool at the foot of a verdant hollow. Stroll on over a stile to a substantial footbridge over another stream. Turn right to cross another bridge and a stile. Follow the path, striking upwards to the left of Alder Hurst End to a stile to a track.

Turn left and walk to Tongue End Farm, taking the signposted gate to the left of the gate across the track. Follow it as it swings right and then rejoins the track beyond the dwelling. Walk into Gilford Clough along the clear track and then out onto open pasture, with the moorland slopes of Boulsworth Hill ahead. Stroll on to a stile to the left of a gate and walk left, along the reinforced track, serenaded by skylarks, meadow pipits and curlews.

This high-level way continues over the moorland, where cotton-grass grows in the damp areas and brooklime thrives in the ditches. At a cross of tracks, continue ahead along the partly paved trod, swinging left as you approach Saucer Hill Clough (a mile and a quarter from where you joined the track). From the rowans scattered over the slopes comes the call of a cuckoo. Look for the Pendle Way sign, directing you downhill right, to cross the stream on stepping stones and continue left. Beyond the stile to the side of the gate continue ahead. Strike left to a

'Clam' bridge, Wycoller

signposted stile, leaving the Pendle Way and joining the Bronte Way.

Head down the slope, to your left the Forest of Trawden - no forest now, but peaceful pastures. Pass through the gate and press on in front of Dean House Farm. Follow the waymarks and walk the reinforced track to join a lane where you continue left. A few yards along, spanning the Wycoller Beck, stands the 'clam' bridge, a single slab of gritstone which probably dates from the Iron Age. It appears precariously balanced on the lane side but is in fact quite firm and safe.

Carry on to Wycoller and then walk the lane up the gentle hill to rejoin your car.

22: Circular walk from Chipping via Dinkling Green

Distance:	9 miles
Time:	5 hours
Parking:	Public car park in Chipping. (It is said that all roads lead to Chipping)
Terrain:	Easy walking all the way. May be muddy by the River Loud after rain. Take care on the Bailey Hippings
Map:	OS Pathfinder 669 SD 64/74, Clitheroe and Chipping, an essential for this walk as there are few signposts

The hamlet of Dinkling Green, a tiny settlement set in a hollow surrounded by limestone knolls, seems at least a couple of centuries behind most of Lancashire. Peace pervades. No motorway and no railway impinges on the quietness of this lovely corner of the Forest of Bowland.

Park in the large village of Chipping, $10^{1}/_{2}$ miles from Garstang. The car park lies close to St Bartholomew's Church, parts of whose fabric date from 1240. Turn right to walk to the front of the splendid church, which you may like to visit. Walk downhill, past the Sun Inn and the end of the aptly named Windy Street. Continue in front of the house of John Brabin, the founder of Chipping School and almshouses. Look for the date, 1668, over the ancient studded door of his old home. Cross Chipping Brook Bridge to see a renovated mill, now a restaurant with the water wheel in situ.

Stroll back to the car park and continue along the road past Berry's chair factory, housed in an old cotton mill. Huge tree trunks wait to be cut on a great saw. Notice the row of cottages opposite, which were once the workhouse. Continue uphill to look over the wall on the left to the mill pond. This tranquil stretch of water, almost surrounded by trees, is home to a pair of mallards with five tiny ducklings - barely more than yellow balls of fluff.

Half way along the pond, take the stile, signposted Burnslack, on the right. Climb straight up the slope, with an ever increasing view of the encircling fells, to a stile in the right-hand corner of the pasture.

Continue ahead to the next stile. Beyond where the indistinct path branches take the right fork and continue over two more stiles to Birchen Lee (built in 1867). Turn right and walk a wide track in the direction of Chipping Lawn. Just before the farm buildings, head off left to keep to the right of a small plantation of conifers, to come to the edge of a wooded gill through which the Leagram Brook descends in many attractive falls. Follow a path, down through the bluebells and saxifrage, to cross a wooden footbridge. Climb out of the gill on the narrow path and walk straight across the pasture to a stile and a gate onto a track. Turn right to pass the ruined Park Style Farm and continue between a row of splendid beech trees.

Remain on the cart-track until you reach Lickhurst Farm. Here, where violets, wild strawberry, wood anemones and wood sorrel flower, turn left and drop down the reinforced track. At the bottom, where primroses blossom, cross the beck on a footbridge. Walk up the slope ahead and follow the stiled and gated indistinct path to pick up a farm-track in the left-hand corner of a pasture.

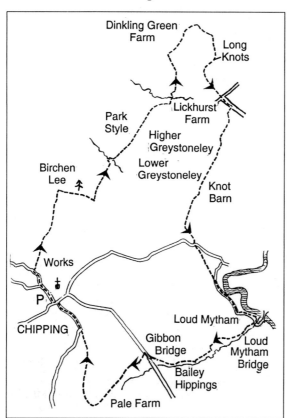

The track brings you at last to Dinkling Green, which is owned by Myerscough Agricultural College. Wander around the buildings. Look for the stone head above one of the barns. Notice the old school-house. Pause in front of the two

*Chipping Church
and hawthorn in bloom*

early seventeenth century cottages with mullioned windows and Tudor doorheads. Peep into the well organised buildings that house the in-lamb sheep. Then, when you can drag yourself away from this lovely corner, walk on along the track, which bears right, to pass below Long Knots to a lane. Cross over and walk along a lane that leads to Chipping, to the track on the right, leading to Higher and then Lower Greystoneley.

Beyond Lower Greystoneley step out along the good track, passing an excellent limekiln just off on the right. At the track end, cross the road and climb the stile opposite. Stroll across the pasture to a stile. Beyond, walk on along the lane, which is lined with hawthorns in blossom, to Loud Mytham Bridge. House martins dive overhead and twittering swallows sit on an overhead wire.

Just before the bridge, take the stile on the right and walk along the stiled bank of the River Loud, passing through primroses, bird's eye, violets, wood anemones and wild strawberry. After three-quarters of a mile cross the Bailey Hippings (stepping stones). Once on the opposite bank continue alongside the delightful Loud to Gibbon Bridge. Climb the ladder stile to the lane which you cross. Walk right to pass the Country House Hotel and the cottage beyond. Take the stile on the left and walk diagonally right across the pastures to Moss Side. Turn left to walk the farm-track to renovated Pale Farm (originally built in 1785). Pass in front of the house to take a stile on the right.

Strike slightly right to a plank across the dyke in the far corner. Continue ahead along the stiled way to Windy Street, Chipping. As you return look out for John Brabin's School and the almshouses.

Mallard and ducklings

23: Circular walk around Slaidburn in the Forest of Bowland

Distance:	6¹⁄₂ miles
Time:	4 hours
Parking:	Public car park and toilets at Slaidburn, by River Hodder
Terrain:	Easy walking all the way. Paths could be muddy after rain
Maps:	OS Pathfinder 660 SD 65/75 Slaidburn & Forest of Bowland
	669 SD 64/74 Clitheroe and Chipping

This walk starts at Slaidburn, which lies in the eastern corner of the Forest of Bowland. It is a village in which to linger to view its Wesleyan Chapel (1889), its fine war memorial, its famous inn, its cobbled pavements and its glorious church of St Andrew's with its box pews and three-tiered pulpit.

The car park is found very close to the River Hodder. Turn right as you leave and walk through the village. Where the road swings right towards Clitheroe, continue straight ahead to walk in front of the Hark to Bounty Inn. Until 1875 it was called the Dog Inn. 'Hark to Bounty' was the comment of a squire who visited the inn in that year and heard his favourite hound Bounty barking.

Continue along Back Lane, with the sturdy stone houses on either side. Walk past a farm with pink cranesbill in flower on its wall. It was built in 1707. Take the footpath on the right, signposted Woodhouse. Walk through the trees to the side of the Croasdale Brook where in spring kingcups and bluebells carpet the woodland floor.

Climb the stile and continue through the trees. Follow the footpath sign that directs you to the left to walk beside a wire fence, over Tenter Hill, to the stepped stone stile in the far corner. Beyond the next stile step over a small stream on a large stone slab. Strike right across the pasture to a gap into another pasture. Walk ahead, keeping the wall to the right and continue where the wall becomes part of a walled track to Myttons. The farm was built in 1846 and it has a huge cobbled yard. One of the barns now houses a craft and teashop.

Follow the track round to the left, and where it swings right pass through a rough stile beside a gate on the left. Walk a few yards to the

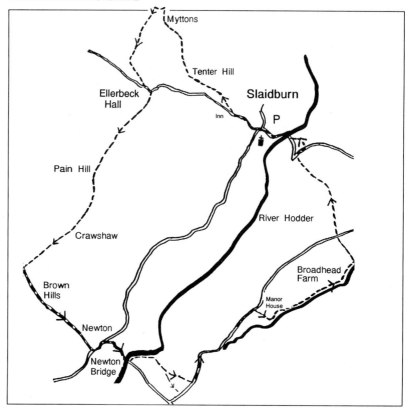

stile on the left and then walk ahead, keeping the wall to the right. Enjoy the utter peace of this lovely area - no traffic or aircraft noise, just the call of curlews and the songs of skylarks. Continue over the next stile and then walk to the left of the straggly hawthorn hedge to a stile ahead. Strike diagonally left to a blue metal gate above the farm buildings. Pass through the next gate to the road and walk left to view Ellerbeck Hall, dated 1694. This grand stone mullioned house sits in a sunny hollow surrounded by rolling pastures.

Continue down the lane to cross a small bridge. Turn right along a track to a gate. Walk ahead to a stile in the wall and continue beside a thorn hedge on the left until you reach Pain Hill, a farm dated 1689. Pass round it to the right to climb a wall stile onto the farm access track. Follow it as it hugs the side of a walled sycamore wood, with a rookery, on the left. Climb a stone stile and continue along the track over the pastures, with green plovers wheeling and diving overhead. Walk on

94

where the track ceases, keeping a walled beech wood to the left. Take a stile into a paddock and walk past Crawshaw Farm to stride along the farm-track to the road.

Turn left and walk past Brown Hills Farm and continue to the village of Newton with its fine sixteenth and seventeenth century houses.

Follow the signpost directions for Clitheroe and walk down to Newton Bridge which crosses the River Hodder. Turn left on the far side to take an unsignposted stile. Stroll beside the hurrying river to cross a stile where a dipper hurries upstream. Turn right and walk the path to a narrow lane. Turn left and stride on to pass Robinsons Farm (1699) and then the stone mulliond Manor House at Easington. Here, in a barn, several pairs of swallows tend their broods - perhaps their third.

Turn right after the last barn and walk between the farm buildings to a track that leads to a small bridge over the Easington Brook. Do not cross but continue along the side of the stream. Here look for oyster catchers snoozing on a pebbly reach. A male redshank, with brilliant red legs, flies downstream uttering its haunting cry and a pair of sandpipers flit from boulder to boulder.

Follow the stream bank round to Broadhead Farm. Pass through the waymarked gates and in front of the house. Continue turning left to walk the farm access track to the narrow road again. Cross, and climb the signposted stile. Walk up the slope, keeping the wall to the left. Climb the stile on the left and continue in the same direction beside a larch plantation. At the bottom of the slope, climb the broken stile and turn left to climb uphill. When you reach the walled copse bear diagonally right to drop downhill to a stone stile onto the road. Cross, turn right and walk to another stile. Beyond, an indistinct path drops downhill and then left to the road bridge over the River Hodder. The car park lies beyond.

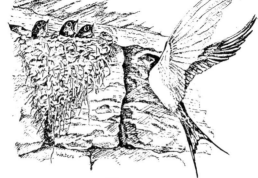

Swallow's nest

24: Circular walk from Holme Chapel

Distance:	4¹/₂ miles
Time:	3 hours
Terrain:	Lots of hills and dales. The climb to the trig. point on Thieveley Pike is very rough walking. Walking boots advisable
Map:	OS Pathfinder 690 SD 82/92 Rawtenstall and Hebden Bridge

This up-and-down-several-times walk starts from Holme Chapel, an unspoilt village set snugly in the magnificent Cliviger Gorge. Dr T.D. Whitaker, the eighteenth century historian of Whalley, a member of the family that lived for several generations at The Holme, planted many of the woodland trees beside which you stroll at the start of the walk. Overlooking all is Thieveley Pike (449m), the highest point of the walk. From its skirts you can look into the village to see the church of St John, with its handsome bell-tower, framed by trees.

The village lies 3 miles south-east of Burnley on the A646. Park in the large lay-by a quarter of a mile south-east, beyond the linear settlement. From here, walk back towards the village and take the first waymarked signpost on the right. Pass through a hand gate on your left that has a signpost beyond. Continue upwards, with the walled woodland of The Holme to your left, to climb steadily through flowering grasses, spangled with bedstraw and tormentil, to a hand gate in the top left corner.

Stride on, with a wall to the right over which you can just see the tips of the propellers of a wind farm. Pass through two hand gates to the right of Light Birks Farm. Turn right and, beyond the next gate, turn immediately left to a stile to join an easier concessionary path. This runs above a wall, avoiding a bull with its cows and calves. Continue beside the stately beeches and riotous rhododendrons of The Holme. Follow the wall to descend to a footbridge over the alder-lined Green Clough, a glorious corner where ragged robin grows in profusion and dog roses turn their pretty pink flowers to the sun.

Climb the stile and, following the waymark, continue beside the walled woodland to another stile. Stroll on to the end of the wall to a third waymarked stile, and follow the arrow to strike diagonally left

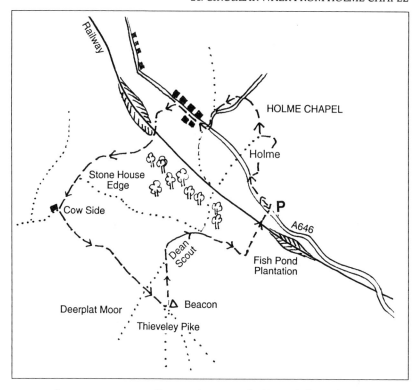

across the pasture to a stile to a farm track. Turn left and walk to the A646. Almost opposite stands the Ram Inn. In fields behind the pub the Lonk Fair is held on the last Saturday in September. Lonks are hardy hill sheep; the rams have large curving horns.

Turn right to walk through the small village and then cross the road to take the signposted track, close to the telephone box. Continue along the track, passing between two dwellings, to walk under the gated railway bridge. Stride ahead to a waymarked post. Here turn right and walk 20 yards to a gate at the corner of two derelict walls. (Do not continue to the waymarked stile.)

Beyond follow a thin path that climbs west, moving away from woodland high on your left. Pass between the steep slopes on your left and a lesser height on your right to pick up a faint grassy track that swings steadily left. Continue bearing uphill, and left, to the waymarked stone steps in the corner where a wire fence joins a wall, high on Stone House Edge.

Before you pass through the gap in the wall, enjoy the extensive view

97

Thieveley Scout and wren

of east Lancashire, with Pendle Hill brooding over pleasing pastures and scattered towns and villages. Then walk ahead across a pasture where Lonk sheep graze, to the back of the buildings of Cow Side. Turn left and walk beside the wall on your right to pass through a gate. Beyond continue to the next gate beside a rusty shed. If the gate is locked you will have to climb it, to continue on the right of way; there is no stile over the wall, or over the wire fence behind it. Stride the reinforced track for 20 yards to cross Black Clough.

To reach the trig. point on Thieveley Pike, a beacon site, leave the track, and continue diagonally right over the tussocks of the rough moorland, the haunt of innumerable carolling skylarks. When you attain the highest point, enjoy the magnificent view that awaits you, ranging for almost 360 degrees over east Lancashire.

From now on the way is nearly all down. Stand with your back to the fence and the derelict ancient boundary wall, which cross the shoulder of the pike, and walk the thin path that leads from the base of the trig. point. As you descend, to cross the good track which you left earlier, look for evidence of past opencast workings. Beyond the track stands a tall waymarked stone directing you along a clear path that winds round to the left of the deep cleft of Dean Scout to a stile. Beyond is a gatepost with four waymarks. Take the stile to the right of the gate and head on along a delightful valley path, keeping close to the wall on your left. Towering to the right are the buttressed sides of Thieveley Scout.

Follow the path as it continues beside a wall to your right to a waymarked post. Here turn sharp left and climb to the top of the slope to another post. Below, you can just discern some patches of blue water among trees and, beyond, your car. Drop down the steep slope to the next post and down an even steeper slope to a waymarked stile, into woodland, below a large sycamore. Continue down the stepped slope, bearing slightly right to reach the good path that skirts the fishpond. A board tells you that this is a landscaped angling facility created from a derelict site.

Turn left and dawdle through this delectable area beneath oaks and birch, where wrens and blackcaps sing. Arrow-heads flower in the pool, fish jump and anglers wait patiently. Follow the track slightly left and then continue as it becomes paved and passes between walls. Cross the footbridge and walk to the road. Turn right and walk 200 yards to rejoin your car.

25: Circular walk from Low Bentham

Distance:	7 miles
Time:	4 hours
Terrain:	Easy walking but after rain many farm-tracks can be muddy
Map:	OS Pathfinder 650 SD 66/76 High Bentham and Clapham

This walk starts in Yorkshire but for most of the way you stroll through the pastures of a quiet corner of Lancashire. The paths link one farm with another and were in use long before today's connecting roads were constructed.

Park in the free car park at Low Bentham, which lies on the south side of Low Bentham Road. Turn left out of the car park and walk west through the delightful village, crossing the bridge over the raging River Wenning, which flows north. Turn left after the Punch Bowl Inn (1670) into Eskew Lane. To the right, unexpectedly, lies the River Wenning again - but now flowing south under a splendid arched bridge. A look at your map solves the puzzle; this is where the river makes a large S-shaped curve.

Walk along the lane to take the stiled footpath, signposted High Bentham, on the left. Continue ahead to pass through a gateless gap keeping to the right of a hedge. Stride up the slope to pass through another gateless gap. Carry on to a signposted stile onto Mill Lane, passing a house, Cloudsbank, on your left. Here you can hear the tremendous noise made by the Wenning negotiating a series of weirs. If you walk left and lean over the white railings you see the tempestuous river make its spectacular descent.

To continue the walk, carry on south along Mill Lane (turn right at the stile to the lane) and take the second signposted way on the right. From the good track you have a grand view of High and Low Bentham. Continue to the courtyard in front of Kirkbeck, a gracious farmhouse dated 1676. Earlier a monastery stood here and its stone was used to construct the farm. Follow the waymark to cross a muddy track to a stone-stepped stile.

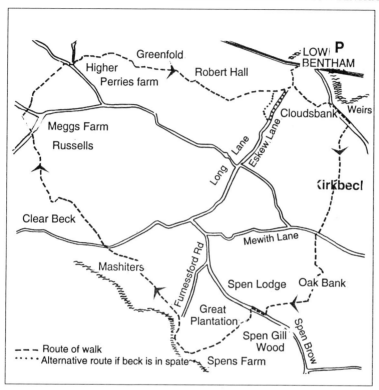

Bear slightly left to cross a wooden footbridge over Eskew Beck and into Lancashire. Climb up the slope through woodland, which is deeply littered with leaves, to a stile. Continue ahead, keeping beside the beck deep in its wooded gill to cross the next stile. Continue beside the Eskew to a stepped stile to Mewith Lane, where harebells flower in profusion. Turn right and take the next left turn, a cart-track, to Oak Bank Farm.

Take the gate on the right at the end of the track and walk right beside a wall in front of the farmhouse. Turn left to a gate just beyond the house. Cross to the far right corner to a white post, a stile and a plank footbridge. Beyond, turn right and walk beneath a row of hawthorns. Pass through a stile to the right of a gate and walk ahead, where flock of wild geese take off from the pasture, rapidly getting into a V-formation as they go. Continue ahead to a stone stile to the left of a gate onto Spen Brow, where you turn right to walk the quiet lane. Bright red glass-like berries of wild bryony trail over the hedgerow bushes.

101

Robert Hall,
Low Bentham.
Crab apple and
harebell

Stroll the lane until you reach Spen Lodge, with its large white studded doors. Take the first of two farm gates on your left and strike left across the pasture to the side of Spen Gill Wood. Look down to the tiny stream, which is almost hidden in the depths of the extremely steep-sided gill. Continue down the gated way to Spens Farm in its delightful wooded hollow. Take the gated stepped-stile on your right and continue beside Great Plantation, over a lush meadow, to a gate to Furnessford Road, where you turn right.

Climb the hill to a signposted footpath leading left into a wood where a green woodpecker calls. Keep to the left of the fence, the boundary between the wood and the farm. Follow the narrow path that keeps well above the River Hindburn to a waymarked stile. Beyond, continue in the same general direction (north-west) to cross two stiled pastures. Drop down the slope to a ladder stile to the right of a reinforced track. Continue ahead to pass to the right of Mashiters and on to Long Lane, which you cross. Walk a few yards left, to a signposted gate.

Continue ahead to a stile in the left corner of the pasture. Continue to the far corner to a rather awkward stile, under a crab apple tree. Beyond, drop downhill to a double clapper bridge over Clear Beck. Turn left through the next gate and walk ahead to the far end of a barn, set in a hidden hollow. Pass through the gate on your right immediately beyond the building and strike diagonally left across the small pasture to a stile. Beyond, follow the raised track that swings slightly left and uphill to a stile beneath an oak. Head on across the pasture to another stile and then bear left and walk to a gate to a lane.

Turn right and pass the farmhouse, Russells (1682). Beyond, turn left into another lane in the direction of Meggs Farm. Once past the farmhouse on your left, pass under the wire on your right and walk to a stile in the corner of the hedge, then ahead to a stone-stepped stile to the access track to a dwelling. Turn left and pass through a small black gate and continue ahead behind the house to a stile in a fence. Bear diagonally right to cross a pasture, where a hare swiftly races away, to a stile half way along the hedge on your right. Beyond, walk ahead to cross two stiles to reach a narrow lane.

Turn right and walk 20 yards to take the signposted footpath on the left to Higher Perries Farm. Turn right beyond the last building to a stile under an oak. Drop down the pasture to the left corner. Walk ahead to a hidden waymarked stile in the hedge and continue slightly right to walk to a gate to Greenfold Farm. Turn right along the farm's access track and then left, following the arrows, to cross two stiles.

Continue, to pass through a gate at the end of the wood on your right and climb uphill to enjoy the ancient Robert Hall, with its mullioned windows and square chimney. It was once a fortified dwelling that belonged to the Harringtons and the Cantsfields. It has a magnificent beamed barn with a huge fireplace and an arch on its north wall, probably from an earlier building on the site. It has a secret priest hole, and for many years had its own chapel and priest. Katherine Parr, later to become Henry VIII's queen, is reputed to have holidayed here.

Continue along the farm-track to pass through a gate on the left of a cattle-grid. Stride diagonally left, keeping to the back of (north of) a ruined barn, to a stile into a wood. Drop down the slope, turn left to ford the Eskew and walk the track beyond to the road. (If the stream is in spate, follow it upstream through the trees and on until you reach the farm's access track to the road, where you turn left.) Continue to the Punch Bowl Inn with its old mounting block. Turn right to rejoin your car.

26: Circular walk from Ribchester

Distance:	5½ miles
Time:	3 hours
Terrain:	Easy walking, but expect plenty of mud, even in June, after rain
Map:	OS Pathfinder 680 SD 63/73 Longridge and Great Harwood

The village of Ribchester is encircled by gently rolling hills and sits on a curve of the River Ribble, from which it takes its name. Travellers used to cross the river here - a dangerous exploit because it flows wide and surging - but swallows and house martins enjoy the spot, delighting in the profusion of insects over its waters on a summer's day.

Beneath the village are the remains of a Roman fort, Bremetannacum, built some time around AD80, and which housed 500 soldiers. Part of the fort lies under the churchyard of the thirteenth century parish church, and just outside its gates is the Roman museum.

Park in the large free visitors' car park and follow the directions for the Roman bathhouse and museum to walk down Church Street. Notice the eighteenth century cottages, particularly those opposite the White Bull. They once housed handloom weavers. The pub has a fine canopy supported by columns and bearing a striking carved wooden bull. Continue past the primary school. Beyond is your first view of the stately swift-flowing Ribble. Turn right to walk the Ribble Way, continuing past the access road to the museum and the church, and through the buildings of a farm.

Stride the hedged track out into the gloriously quiet Lancashire countryside. Look across the river, which is tucked in a fold of pasture, to Osbaldeston Hall, a majestic Elizabethan house. Continue past a small house, with a large barn. It was once the home of the ferryman who carried people across the river to the hall. Pass through the kissing gate beside a farm gate and continue ahead, with a delightful view of the now very wide hurrying Ribble to your left. On the far bank stands a heron, waiting patiently for fish.

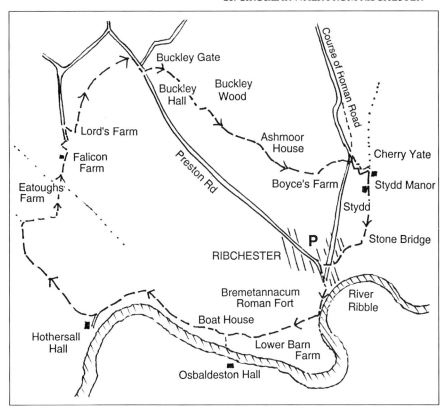

Beyond the next stile, pass below ash and sycamore, from where a brilliantly coloured male woodpecker flies off. Continue to the next kissing gate and climb the steep slope which, lined with tall beeches, begins to drop down to the Ribble. From here enjoy the view of the curving river, flowing through green pastures, and walk on to climb a ladder stile and continue to Hothersall Hall, which was rebuilt in 1856. Beyond, high on a farm building, a stone plaque carries the initials T.H. and the date 1695, all that remains of the original manor house.

Follow the Ribble Way sign to ascend a concrete access track, which you leave by a gate on the right after a hundred yards. Climb the reinforced track up the slope and continue ahead over the next pasture to a gate in the left corner. Walk ahead to pass through a tall deer gate to stride between more deer netting to a hedged track that swings right to Ox Hey. Here turn left and, opposite the dwelling, walk right beyond a waymarked gate.

Head on along the continuing track to straddle a waymarked stile where you turn left to walk to a footbridge over a narrow gutter. Follow the gutter left and then right. Pass between a pond and the hedge and then strike right. Eatoughs Farm lies on your left and you take a gate in the far right corner. This gives access to a pleasingly hedged track, where you turn left.

Follow the track as it swings right and then drops down a slope bordered with red campion and huge golden buttercups. Pass the access track to Falicon Farm. Continue past two more dwellings and then turn right to walk towards Lord's Farm. Just inside the entrance gate turn left and pass through two gates. Continue between farm buildings and on to take the left of two gates where you continue beside the fence on your right. Then take the second gate on the right and continue in the same direction. Here green plovers and curlews nest.

Climb the broken stile in the left corner between two scrubby hawthorns. Walk ahead to cross a small footbridge and then continue ahead to a gate to Preston Road, where you turn right. Walk on until you see the signposted footpath on the other side of the road beyond Green Moor Lane.

Stride yet another track, with pleasing views across the pastures, to pass in front of Buckley Hall. Beyond strike diagonally left across a buttercup pasture to a stile in the corner of Buckley Wood. Drop down the slope through the lovely woodland to cross the footbridge over Boyce's Brook into a secluded, quiet hollow beside the stream. Follow the brook downstream to a footbridge over a feeder stream and then bear left to ascend the slope, where ragged robin grows in a wet flush. Pass below birch and continue climbing to pass through hawthorns and then bear right. Keep to the left of Ashmoor house and beyond join its access track.

Head on along it towards Boyce's Farm. At the end of the second barn, and before the farmhouse, turn left to climb the stile in the corner of the fence. Keep to the left of a pond and then continue to a broken footbridge at the left end of a row of willows. Beyond, climb the slope and continue ahead to a stile to Stonygate Lane, opposite Cherry Yate, which has an attractive staircase window. Look for the name and datestone, 1684, set in the wall of the house.

Turn left and take the signposted stile on the right. Drop diagonally right to cross a small stream and continue to a red gate into Stydd Manor Farm. A stone over its front door carries the date 1698. Pass through

*Buckley Hall, Ribchester
and sycamore*

another red gate and walk towards the lovely old Stydd Church, with its Norman doorway and north facing windows. Continue to pass Stydd almshouses, which were endowed in 1726 by John Shireburn for Catholic women. They were refurbished in 1962 and are still maintained by the Catholic church.

Walk on to Stone Bridge an the Blackburn Road. Turn right and walk into Ribchester, hopefully leaving yourself time to explore the charming village.

27: Walk from Longridge

Distance:	7¹/₂ miles
Time:	3-4 hours
Terrain:	Easy walking, but some tracks can be very muddy after rain and if the cattle are still in the pastures. Wellingtons or strong boots advisable
Map:	OS Pathfinder 680 SD 63/73 Longridge and Great Harwood

This is a walk which takes you through the tranquil countryside that lies between Longridge Town and the stately River Ribble. In autumn the hedgerows are a riot of colour and laden with berries. A few summer flowers linger on beneath the hazels, thorns and ashes. Across the Ribble the tall forest trees are a blaze of yellow, gold and saffron and excited jays call from sturdy oaks as they gorge on acorns.

This sylvan, pastoral walk starts from the car park of the Duke William pub where walkers are welcome to park. Opposite stands the pleasing church of St Lawrence with St Pauls, built in 1822, its fine tower added in 1841. Walk right along the B6243 and turn left beside the church, following the bridlepath sign to walk Chapel Brow. Stride the narrow road, past Lamplighter Cottage, into the peaceful pastures, south of the busy small town.

Walk the cobbled way that passes between the Alston reservoirs - alas, there is no view of their waters. At the T-junction of tracks, bear left to stroll the hedged way where long tailed tits flit gracefully through hawthorn, spindle and hazel. Continue along the track as it bears right and right again by Bury's Farm. Head on to pass another farm and then on in the same direction to Manor House. As you pass through the pastures, look for the many ponds, fringed with reeds and often shadowed by hawthorns. These are marl pits from where clay for brick-making has been obtained.

At Manor Farm the track swings right and becomes concreted. Walk to the cattle-grid and turn left into a well kept hedged way, in the direction of Jenkinson's Farm. Just before the entrance, turn right to walk another track to Higher Yew Tree Farm (there is now no trace of the yew tree), passing two old marker stones, and then another, directing

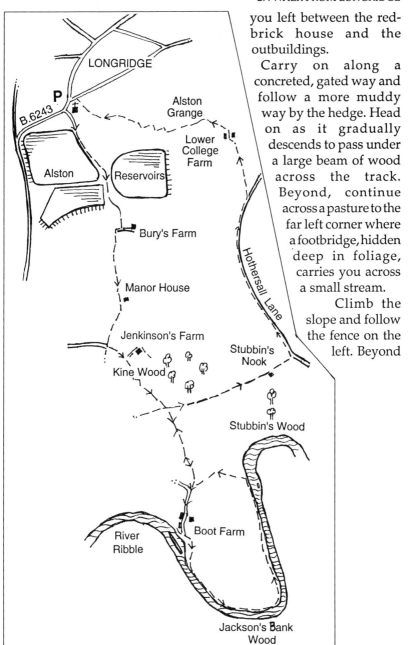

you left between the red-brick house and the outbuildings.

Carry on along a concreted, gated way and follow a more muddy way by the hedge. Head on as it gradually descends to pass under a large beam of wood across the track. Beyond, continue across a pasture to the far left corner where a footbridge, hidden deep in foliage, carries you across a small stream.

Climb the slope and follow the fence on the left. Beyond

109

stand several cherry trees covered with brilliant red leaves. By following the fence you reach the signposted stile, again hidden deep in a luxuriant hedgerow. Stride the lane ahead to pass Boot Farm. Continue on the hedged track beyond, that leads you to the side of the wide, surging River Ribble.

Turn left, climb the stile and begin the pleasing stroll along the river where it makes a large U-shaped meander. Look for a charm of goldfinches feasting on a large clump of burdock as you head upstream. Several herons fly over the pastures to the left and descend to the far bank to begin fishing. Jackson's Bank Wood clothes the steep slopes opposite and the trees are arrayed in autumnal glory. A small group of cormorants take off from a dead branch overhanging the peaty river.

The bird life along this stretch of the river is fascinating but even more riveting are the great stands of Himalayan balsam now laden with elegant pink flowers - except for figwort they have crowded out all other flowers. Head on along the stiled way. Look far left to see, on a small hill, Alston Hall and its observatory. At the edge of Stubbin's Wood, climb the stile and head right across the pasture to a stile in the top signposted corner. Walk on along the continuing track to cross a bridge and take the signposted stile in the hedge on the right, which you climbed earlier.

Follow the fence on your right all the way to the footbridge, cross to the far left corner of the pasture to pass under the barrier and climb the track beyond. Three hundred and fifty yards along look for the insignificant Ribble Way signs on a stile on your right. Cross and walk ahead to the next stile and drop down the slope, to the left of the hedge, to a footbridge in King Wood. Climb the slope, with a strip of woodland to your left and an extensive view of the lovely Ribble valley to your right. Walk the stiled way to pass behind Stubbin's Farm to the quiet Hothersall Lane. Turn left and walk for three-quarters of a mile, to take the fifth footpath (not all signposted) on the left, where a two-armed signpost directs you towards 'Blackburn Road, one mile'.

Continue, in the same general direction, across a wet rough pasture to a stile in the middle of the fence, and then on to the gate in the boundary fence of Lower College Farm. Beyond the gate, turn left and then right between derelict farm buildings that once belonged to a Cambridge college. Walk in front of the farmhouse to a ladder stile. Beyond, turn left and walk to another. Beyond, swing right across the pasture to pass through a waymarked gate. Turn left and follow the hedge to drop down through the trees of College Wood to cross a footbridge.

Goldfinch on burdock

Climb from the bridge to a stile out of the trees. Walk across the pasture to a stile to a track. Turn right towards Alston Grange. Keep left of the farm buildings to reach another track, where you turn left. Follow it right. Turn left and walk ahead between two of several large farm buildings to a stile to a pasture. Cross the pasture to a stile beside the blue gate on the right of two. Walk the walled and hedged track and continue to the gate on the left to walk through the churchyard to visit St Lawrence's. From here, at last, you can see the waters of Alston reservoirs.

28: Figure-of-eight walk from Bolton-by-Bowland

Distance:	First walk 3 miles
	Second walk 4½ miles
Time:	2-3 hours & 3½ hours
Terrain:	Easy walking all the way
Map:	OS Pathfinder 669 64/74 Clitheroe and Chipping

On a pleasant Saturday in October it is often difficult to find peace and quiet in this busy county of ours, where most leisure activities produce noise. Stroll the glorious countryside that surrounds tranquil Bolton-by-Bowland to enjoy a quietness that is broken only by bird-song. This walk can be completed as one or it can be done in two parts with a break for lunch in the village.

Park in the car park close to Skirden Bridge at the west end of the village. Walk through the village to the smaller of Bolton's two greens. Pause by the latter to look at the stocks, a millstone and the stump of an old market cross. Walk along the road, signposted Gisburn, crossing a small bridge over the Kirk Beck. To the left stands the church of St Peter and St Paul, with its magnificent tower. Inside, the walls are of unrendered stone and the pews of oak. Enter the small chapel and look for the memorial slab to Sir Ralph Pudsay, who rebuilt the church in the fifteenth century. Here, carved in stone, you can see Ralph, his three wives and his 25 children.

Walk on to the larger second green to see the old courthouse and its weather-vane. Here the village school looks towards the church over the greensward. Walk back to the large gate opposite the church, now the entrance to the track to Bolton Hall Farm. Once it led to the now demolished Bolton Hall, home of Sir Ralph.

Pass through the signposted gate and walk the tree-lined avenue, climbing gently through pleasing parkland. Continue through two gateposts, without a gate, and notice the remains of an ancient cross on the left. Stroll through two more gateposts to turn left before a gate across the drive. Continue climbing steadily to a stile in the right corner, from where there is a grand view of Ingleborough. Walk ahead to the

112

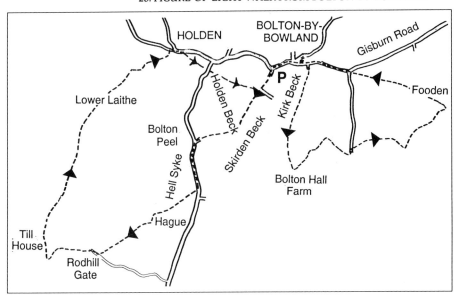

next gate and beyond turn right to walk to a farm gate. To the right stands Pendle Hill, a benevolent giant in sunshine.

Walk the track beyond the gate, bearing left, and then turn right to walk a wide track between the two dwellings at Scott Laithe. Pass through the farm buildings and out into pasture, walking slightly right to a gate where two hedgerows join. Stride diagonally right to a gate in the far right corner. Beyond, drop downhill, keeping the fence to the left to pass through a gate. Climb the stile on your left, 20 yards ahead, and continue left below ash, oak and elm that clothe the steep bank that slopes down the River Ribble.

Continue ahead at the next stile to join an old grassy way lined with thorn bushes. Look for the broken stile obscured by a hawthorn bush at the end, beyond which lies the hamlet of Fooden. Walk left of the barn and pass through a gate. Bear right and then strike left across the pasture to a white-painted stile, which you climb. Stroll the pasture, continuing in the same direction, to an unusual stile in the top right corner. Beyond, bear left to cross a stile under an oak. Continue across the pasture to a signposted gate to the road. Turn left to walk into Bolton-by-Bowland.

Walk through the village, past the car park, to cross the bridge over Skirden Beck and take the access track on the left. Walk the lovely lane and where the track swings left, take the well signposted stile on the right. Climb the slope, following the directions for Sawley, to pass the remains of another ancient cross. Drop down the slope to a waymarked stile at the bottom. Beyond, strike diagonally right almost to the far right corner to straddle a stile over a fence. Walk ahead to cross, under alders, a sturdy footbridge over Holden Beck, where a heron feeds. Climb the steep slope ahead to a signposted gap stile to reach Sawley Road. Turn left to walk past Bolton Peel, a splendid Elizabethan farmhouse, with an ancient cross in front of it and a bank barn to its far side.

Stroll the hedged road for a quarter of a mile to take an unsignposted gate on the right, opposite a gate and a track on your left. Keep beside the boundary on your right to cross Hell Syke, with a stride, to a stile on the other side. Strike diagonally left across the pasture to pass through a gate to Hague Farm. Walk left through the buildings and notice the dovecote and weather-vane on the end of the barn on the right. Pass through the gate to the lane and turn immediately right through another gate. Strike diagonally left to pass through a gate. Cross a narrow ditch and continue on the same left diagonal to a stile in the corner. Climb the slope, in the same direction, to join a reinforced track left of Rodhill Gate. From here there is a pleasing view of Sawley and of Bolton-by-Bowland.

Continue climbing the track to just beyond where it swings left. Here follow a waymark directing you right to a waymarked stile, on the right of Slipping Brook Barn. Strike diagonally left, climbing towards the top left corner of the pasture, to join a waymarked rough track which continues left. Look for the waymarked gate up a short slope on the right and pass through. Continue up the pasture to a waymarked gate to a lane. Turn right to walk the arrowed way between Till House and the barn to its right. From here, high on the ridge, there is a wonderful view of Ribblesdale.

Take the stile, on the right, behind the far end of the barn and walk the waymarked path to climb two stiles. Beyond, the waymarks cease but continue in the same direction, keeping a fence to the left, to climb a stile. Pass through the next two gates and continue to walk to the right of a barn, Lower Laithe, passing through a splendid gated stile. Stride on to the next gate. Beyond, drop downhill, walking a path in a grassy groove to a gap in the electric fence. Pass through a gate in the hedge just beyond. Stride ahead across the pasture, remaining on the right of a projecting hedge to the lower green gate. Pass through and walk diagonally left to join a farm-track where you turn right. If the electric fence along the track is live, continue to the bottom left corner to a gate giving access to the track.

Pass through Holden Green Farm and carry on to the road. Turn right to walk through the village of Holden. Look for the cottage dated 1687 and the commemorative seat on the small grassed bridge over the Holden Beck. Continue along the road for 50 yards. Pass under a large sycamore and just before some garages, look for the gap stile in the stone wall to your right. Stride ahead to the gap stile opposite and beyond, turn left to climb another. Stroll ahead, remaining on the right of the wall to climb a stile in the left corner onto Sawley Road. Cross and walk the well signposted footpath through Lower Copy Nook Farm. Head on to a stile left of a gate. Follow a grassy track to the left of trees to a stile to the right of a gate. Turn left to the stile taken first at the beginning of the walk. Stride the lane to rejoin your car.

29: Circular walk from Garstang via Grize Dale

Distance:	8 miles
Time:	4-5 hours
Terrain:	Easy walking all the way
Map:	OS Pathfinder 668 SD 44/54 Garstang

This walk starts at Garstang and explores the glorious contryside that lies to the east of the M6 and the railway. The route crosses lush meadows full of cattle and sheep, comes beside two tranquil reservoirs, edges moorland bronzed with dying bracken, passes through lovely autumnal woods and returns beside the pleasing River Wyre.

Park in the car park between the town hall and the town's playing fields. Leave by the paved path that edges the fields, walking beside the River Wyre, which flows to your right. Climb the steps onto the bridge (part of a dismantled railway) to cross the hurrying water. Take the waymarked path on your left to follow a stiled path across pastures to a track, Lingart Lane, where you turn right. Continue until you reach Hazelhead Lane. Turn left and continue past an access track to Higher Lingart Farm to take a signposted footpath on the right. Continue ahead to cross the railway line - with great care - and then a bridge over the M6.

Walk straight ahead across a meadow to a stile onto Keeper's Lane. Stride left along the narrow hedged lane that leads into the glorious Lancashire countryside. Ignore the first left turn and at the next T-junction turn left to walk another lane. From here there is a grand view to Black Combe, Morecambe Bay and Blackpool Tower. After passing a track marked private, take the signposted footpath on the right, opposite the end of a small plantation on your left.

Cross a footbridge on the left and then, to your right, take a stiled footbridge, under willows with long yellow leaves. Walk ahead with the fence to your right. Climb the stile in the right corner of the pasture, turn left beyond a barn and then turn right twice to pass Burns Farm. Turn left, up the farm-track, where a flock of long tailed tits dance through the branches of an old oak.

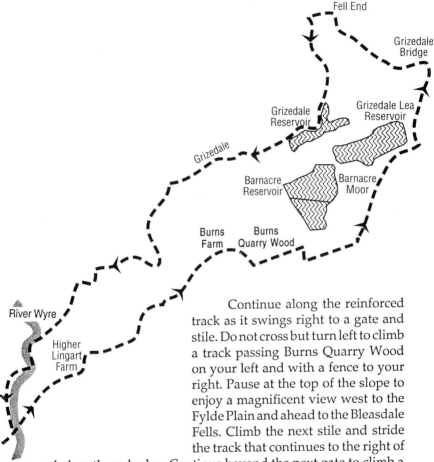

Continue along the reinforced track as it swings right to a gate and stile. Do not cross but turn left to climb a track passing Burns Quarry Wood on your left and with a fence to your right. Pause at the top of the slope to enjoy a magnificent view west to the Fylde Plain and ahead to the Bleasdale Fells. Climb the next stile and stride the track that continues to the right of a straggly hawthorn hedge. Continue beyond the next gate to climb a slope and follow the track where it swings right. Beyond the stile walk left to walk a grassy track lined with foxgloves and willowherb.

Pass Moor House (1866) and continue ahead along a reinforced track towards a wireless station. Just before the station gate, turn left to walk a grassy track, with Barnacre reservoirs coming into view. Late meadow pipits flit about the yellow grass of the pasture. Climb the stile to the right of two gates. To the east stretch the Bleasdale Fells. Head on past the mixed conifer plantation, which is alive with the calls of coal tits and goldcrests.

Follow the track as it begins to descend. A sturdy wall to your left

Grize Dale

encloses Grizedale Lea reservoir, from where comes the quacking of ducks. Far across the plain to your left you can see the white buildings of Lancaster University set in green meadows. Follow the good track to the stile to Delph Lane.

Turn left and walk the moorland road to cross Grizedale Bridge over Grizedale Brook. Turn left to walk the signposted bridleway, passing through two gates. Follow the track as it swings right, with a wall to your right, to pass through the next gate. Beyond, carry on to the far left corner to pass through a gate and walk on between two large barns to the track at Fell End Farm. Here you turn left. Where the track swings right take the gated track on the left, signposted to Grize Dale. Cross a footbridge and continue to a stile and gate into splendid beech woodland.

The good track through the sylvan splendour is a joy to walk. Rhododendrons support fat green buds. Bird-song fills the air. And through the riotously coloured trees there are pleasing glimpses of Grizedale reservoir. Ignore the right turn to Nicky Nook - perhaps promising yourself to walk that way another time. Continue beside the tranquil water and on past the dam. Pass through a kissing gate and walk beside the steep gill. Dawdle through a lovely hollow where steep slopes sweep down to the track and continue to the four-armed signpost where you walk ahead to Higher Lane.

Turn left and carry on to pass Throstle Nest Farm. Cross a ford and climb the hill to cross another (both have footbridges). Beyond, turn right to walk a track on the edge of Long Crossey Wood, with Grizedale Brook chuckling below. Beyond the next gate, the track leads to a bridge over the motorway. Follow the track as it swings left and then right to a kissing gate. Beyond, cross the railway line, and bear left to the corner of Hazelhead Lane. Walk right and take the stile in the hedge on the left, just before a bridge over the brook.

Walk ahead, keeping the alder-lined brook to your right, to follow the waymarked path. Walk to the confluence of the Grizedale with the Wyre and continue left along the clear waymarked path, where you are asked to keep dogs under close control. Walk past a white painted aqueduct and cross the footbridge beyond. Walk to the road. Continue right and take the signposted footpath on the left. Carry on along the bank of the Wyre until you rejoin the paved path round the playing field to the car park.

30: Circular walk from Martin Mere via Mere Sands Wood

Distance:	5½ miles
Time:	Walking time 3 hours
Terrain:	Easy walking all the way
Map:	OS Pathfinder 699 SD 41/51 Chorley and Burscough Bridge

Martin Mere, a large lake, once covered 15 square miles. Through the centuries the low-lying land, much of it below sea level, was gradually drained for agriculture. A small portion was never successfully drained and in 1972 the Wildfowl and Wetlands Trust bought it and established a centre. Here the walk begins. It continues to Mere Sands Wood nature reserve, which is owned and managed by the Lancashire Wildlife Trust. The reserve stands on layered sand and peat. The sand was extensively quarried between 1974 and 1982 for glass-making and then the extraction companies landscaped the site and created a nature reserve.

The Martin Mere Wildfowl and Wetlands Centre lies 6 miles north of Ormskirk and 10 miles south-east of Southport. Leave your car in the car park and walk right along Fish Lane and the continuing Tarlscough Lane, which is lined with ash and poplar. Vast flat pastures stretch away on both sides, the vista nearly treeless and hedgeless. Overhead long skeins of geese head for their feeding grounds and in a ploughed pasture dozens of green plover probe the newly turned earth.

Turn left into Curlew Lane, where workers gather a huge crop of cabbages from almost black soil. Stride on past an extensive crop of carrots and then another of swedes. Follow the narrow lane as it swings right and becomes Tootle Lane. Here grow acres of brussel sprouts. Pass Mere End Farm to take the signposted footpath on the left to walk a private road. Follow the continuing track as it bears right and comes to a footbridge over Rufford Boundary Sluice. Turn right to walk through beech and rhododendrons, part of woodland planted in the mid-nineteenth century by Lord Hesketh.

Just before the end of the wood, turn left to follow the waymarked

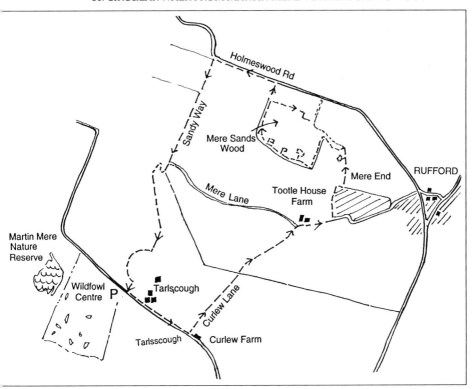

nature trail, passing through birch and Scots pine, where you might see a red squirrel. To the left a path edged with timber leads to Mere End hide. Here look for coot, goldeneye, shoveler and pochard. Carry on through the glorious woodland, almost to the boundary, to bear left and then to take a footpath off left, waymarked, which continues beside a ditch. To the left through the trees you can glimpse Mere End again and to the right the reed-fringed End Lake.

Cross a rustic bridge over the ditch and stroll right to cross a second bridge. Look for bird boxes of varying size fixed to trees. Bear right to cross another bridge and turn right to view the spectacular Tower Hide. This is a 'members only' hide for viewing Heath Lake and End Lake. It was opened by Lord Hesketh in 1989.

Return to the path and walk on through the trees. Ignore the bridge on your left and, just before the next one, turn right to enter the Rufford hide. From here you look out on Inner Twin lake to see mallard, teal, gadwall, coot, cormorant and a pair of great crested grebes performing

Cottage on the vast, flat pasture

part of their courtship ritual. This tranquil arm of a large area of water is surrounded with birch laden with golden leaves, and edged with yellowing grass.

Return to the main path and cross the bridge. Beyond and to the right stands Redwing hide, from where you can see more grebes and perhaps a flash of petrol blue, revealing a kingfisher. Rejoin the path and turn right to cross another bridge. As you near the western boundary, follow the way as it swings right, keeping to the left of the Outer Twin Lake. Stroll on to the northern boundary and notice a stone bearing a '3'. Continue right to stride the path that eventually, after passing Ainscough and further on Marshall hide, comes to the car park and visitor centre. Here you might want to ask about the daily bird count.

Walk back along the path to the stone bearing a '3' and leave the reserve by a narrow path on your right. Cross a plank bridge over a ditch. Strike across the pasture to the signposted gap in the hedge onto Holmeswood Road. Turn left and walk for 700 yards to turn left into Sandy Way. The delightful lane, lined with alders, leads out into the flat arable land once again.

Cross a narrow bridge over the boundary sluice, and beyond, where the lane swings sharp left, walk ahead over the field to cross a footbridge over a dyke. Turn right to walk to another bridge, which you cross. From here look ahead to an old windmill. Turn left and continue to a waymarked stile on your left. Beyond, walk to a board carrying an arrow and a request that you keep to the path. Walk in the direction of the arrow towards a marker post. This directs you left to walk a pleasing raised track, with a ditch beside it, through a huge pasture. At the end of the track bear right, towards a small brick cottage, to walk a track that passes in front of it. Then take a grassy track off right that leads to Fish

Lane.

Turn right and then cross the road to take the footpath to the Wildfowl and Wetlands Centre. The centre is open daily from 9.30am to 5.30pm in summer, 4.00pm in winter. It is closed on December 24 and 25. If you have timed your walk well you will still be able to see the flamingos, view the many and varied ducks, and in the winter, watch the comings and goings of a huge number of Bewick's and Whooper swans. You will find much to do and to see and there is a small restaurant. All admission money goes directly to conserving wetland environments. Don't forget your binoculars!

Eider and other ducks at Martin Mere

31: Circular walk via the Leeds and Liverpool Canal and Harrock Hill

Distance:	7¹/₂ miles
Time:	3-4 hours
Terrain:	Easy walking all the way
Map:	OS Pathfinder 699 SD 41/51 Chorley and Burscough Bridge

Harrock Hill stands tall above the low-lying land of west Lancashire, giving dramatic views, on a good day, of the Welsh mountains and those of the Lake District. It is through this low-lying land that the Leeds and Liverpool Canal has been cut. This walk links the hill with the low land, passing through gentle pastures on the way.

Park on the A5209, 2¹/₂ miles east of Parbold or a quarter of a mile west of Dangerous Corner (1¹/₂ miles west of the M6). Leave your car on the north side of the road, where the remains of the old road are used for parking. Walk towards Parbold for 50 yards, then cross the busy A road to follow a signposted footpath into the glorious Fairy Glen, through which runs Sprodley Brook. The path passes under beech still heavily laden with bronzed leaves. Look for the footpath sign on the left, directing you over a stile and down well fenced steps to climb another stile close beside the hurrying stream. Turn right and walk through the magnificent woodland. Look back to see a pretty waterfall.

Carry on beside the brook, where pink campion still flowers. Cross the footbridge over the water and continue, with a lovely gorge to your right. On reaching a metalled lane, walk downhill beside Delf House Wood. Just before the farm ahead, look for the easy-to-miss stile on your left and stride the continuing footpath, with a hedge to your right. Cross a track, climb the steps opposite and walk ahead to another stile. Head on over the pasture to a lane. Here turn right for 20 yards and then left to continue along a grassy way, in the same general direction, to Appley Lane North, where you turn right.

Cross the railway bridge and press on over a blue bridge, number 42, over the canal. Drop down right to the towpath, which soon takes you out into the rolling Lancashire countryside. Dawdle past a canal lock with deciduous woodland on the opposite bank. Look here for a flash of petrol blue where a kingfisher darts upstream to alight on an overhanging branch. As it settles and turns towards the water its red breast provides perfect camouflage among the red leaves of bramble.

Stride on along the pleasing towpath past bridge 41 and on to bridge 40, which you cross. Walk the continuing track through trees. Cross the stone railway bridge and walk to a T-junction of tracks where you turn

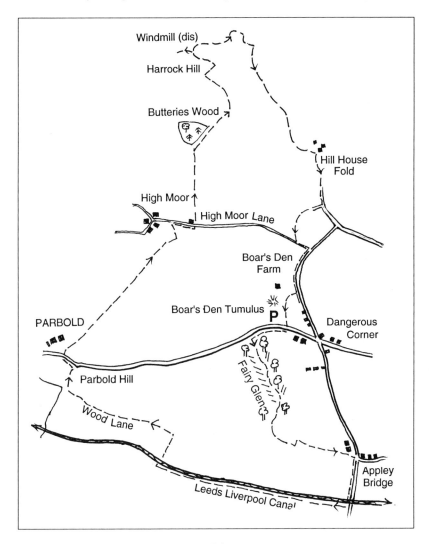

left to stroll along the glorious Wood Lane (a track). After walking for just over half a mile, climb a hidden stile on the right, immediately before the start of houses on the right. Climb the steepish slope to a stile onto the busy Parbold Hill (the A5209 again).

Cross with care and turn left to walk 200 yards to take a track on the right. The footpath sign stands 10 yards in and is very easy to miss. (Do not take the track just beyond, which drops down into the wood.) Climb through the oaks and sycamores to a stile to a pasture. Continue ascending steadily, with a wooded gill to your left from where come the raucous calls of jays. Follow the narrow path as it swings left, still beside the gill, to a stile over a fence. Beyond, strike diagonally right to a stile left of a gate, below an oak, giving access to an attractive track.

Stride ahead, passing to the left of a plantation. Follow the track as it swings right and becomes the tarmacked Broadhay Lane. At the T-junction, cross and turn right to walk along High Moor Lane. Just beyond the restaurant of the same name, turn left into a private road. It is a signposted right of way in the direction of Harrock Hall. Continue to where the access road swings sharp left and follow the stiled footpath ahead - marked with surely the biggest footpath sign ever!

Walk the fenced and hedged track, with Butteries Wood to the left, and then through a small plantation. At the track end, turn sharp left and, with the trees now to your left, walk to the stile in the corner of the pasture. Beyond, walk down the slope with the fence to your right to the next stile. Stroll on to cross the next one. Then walk right and left to edge the pasture to cross a stile into the bracken slopes and woodland of Harrock Hill.

Here make a short diversion left to see a ruined windmill, the remains now carefully stabilised. What splendid isolation the miller had and what a view. Return to the stile and this time (assuming you start with your back to it) walk right. The descending way becomes cobbled and a joy to walk - obviously a sturdy route for carts to the mill. Pass a house on the left and then continue for 150 yards to a house on the right. Here turn right, before the house, to walk the track. Pass behind the next house. Aim for the left of two gaps in the hedge ahead. Beyond, walk on in the same direction, with a deep gill to the left, to join a cart track, along which you stride.

Carry on to climb two stiles and join another farm-track. Ignore the continuing signposted footpath and turn left to walk the stiled track to a lane to the right of Hill House Fold. Turn right to walk the quiet way beside a small copse on the left. Turn right at the next footpath sign and stride the access track until it swings right. At this point continue ahead to a stile in the corner of the fence ahead. Stride on to the next stile and beyond, follow the narrow path as it swings left to join High Moor Lane. Turn left and then right onto a busy road in the direction of Parbold. Walk on to take a signposted track on the right. To the left is a large fishing pond surrounded with trees which host a flock of chattering fieldfares.

Just before Boar's Den Farm take the signposted stile on the left to continue beside the pond. Look right to see a mound - Boar's Den tumulus. Pass through the gap ahead and stride on to a stile, under an oak, to the A5209. Turn right to rejoin your car.

Kingfisher and bramble

127

32: Circular walk from Garstang via Cabus Nook

Distance:	8 miles
Time:	4 hours
Terrain:	Easy walking but some farm-tracks can be very muddy if stock are still in the pastures and returning to be milked
Map:	OS Pathfinder 668 SD 44/54 Garstang

Autumn is a perfect time to walk the gloriously peaceful towpath beside the Lancaster Canal, to cross the well drained mosses north-west of Garstang and to stride the quiet Thorough Way, a haven for hundreds of fieldfare feasting on the fruit-laden hedgerow trees.

Start your walk by turning right out of Parkhill Road car park, Garstang, to pass in front of The Wheatsheaf. At the small roundabout follow the signpost directions for the canal basin. Turn right to walk in front of the Farmer's Arms Hotel and continue to the canal bridge, number 62. To reach the towpath, drop down the steps on the far left side and pass under the pleasing Rennie Bridge.

Stroll the path, where the leaves of willows are now bright lemon. Continue beneath a striking white bridge carrying a huge pipe. It is bridge 63A and was built in 1927 by the Fylde Water Board to carry water from Barnacre reservoir to Blackpool and its surrounds. Continue under two more bridges, 63B and 64. Beyond lies the delightful Lancashire countryside. Continue past the Garstang marina, where innumerable boats are tied up for the winter.

Stride on until you reach brick abutments - all that remains of bridge 65. Before it was demolished it carried the 'Pilling Pig', the Garstang-Knott End Railway. Continue to the second stile on the left, where you leave the towpath. Beyond, look left to see a well preserved limekiln and then pass between the wartime tank traps to a gate to a track in front of Nateby Hall Farm. Turn left and follow the track between the outbuildings, continuing to a waymark pointing right just beyond a small clump of trees, 50 yards beyond the farm.

The waymark directs you to a footbridge over Lee Brook. Walk

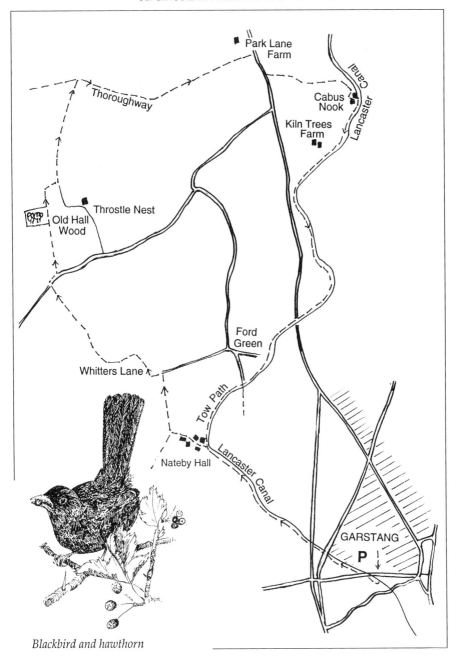

Blackbird and hawthorn

ahead to a stile set in a hawthorn hedge onto Whitters Lane, from where there is a good view of Winmarleigh Hall, standing red-bricked and gracious among its deciduous woodland. This was once the home of the Patten family and is now part of Lancashire College of Agriculture. Turn left and walk the narrow traffic-free lane. Continue past Whitters Hill Farm and at the T-junction turn right into Church Lane. Turn left to climb between the rails of a huge metal gate to walk to the left of the long straight ditch (Lee Brook).

The elderly stile, which you cross to continue, lies in the hedgerow close beside the brook. Walk on beside the brook where wagtails strut along its muddy edges. Stroll beside Old Hall Wood - where several stiles were missing when the author last visited the area - and walk to a stile, totally overgrown with vegetation, in the corner of the hedgerow ahead. Turn right onto a wide lane where in spring the blackthorn bushes are a cloud of white blossom. Where the track swings right to Throstle Nest, turn left and continue over the wide flat marshland beside the brook.

Black Combe lies ahead. Climb the next stile. Continue past the gas terminal, where there are excellent stiles, to turn right to cross a good bridge over Crawley's Dyke. Stride the reinforced Thorough Way, through colourful hedgerows where fieldfares, mistles, redwings and

Limekiln

130

blackbirds feast on the berries of elder, hawthorn and rose. Goldfinches settle in a crowd on burdock and late house martins skim along between the low growing trees.

At Park Lane turn right and walk, with care, 50 yards to the car park of the Patten Arms. Turn left, as directed by the signpost, and walk beside the fence to a footbridge over Park Lane Brook. Continue ahead, bearing to the right of a small pool, one of the many water filled marl pits from which clay was extracted for making bricks. Continue in the same direction to a stile in the hedge and then on the same slightly right diagonal to a gate. Beyond, continue beside the fence to a track, where you turn right. Walk the sometimes muddy gated way to Cabus Nook Farm. Here the right of way passes to the right of the farm but the farmer is quite happy for you to continue on the track. Follow the track as it swings left to a gate onto the towpath. Turn right to pass under bridge 73.

From now on the towpath leading you back to Garstang takes you through tranquil pastures with dramatic views of the Bleasdale Moors away to the left. Look right to see Kiln Trees Farm, where bricks would have been made. Dawdle along the way, where late summer flowers thrive, sheltered by the hedgerows. Pass under more charming bridges and envy those boat owners who have time to travel the waterway. Enjoy the herons that feed, the mallards that squabble and the moorhens that scurry over water and land alike, as you return to Garstang.

33: Circular walk from Higher Hodder Bridge

Distance:	7 miles
Time:	3-4 hours
Terrain:	Easy walking all the way - but in November, and after rain, most cart-tracks are very muddy
Maps:	OS Pathfinder 669 SD 64/74 Clitheroe and Chipping
	680 SD 63/73 Longridge and Great Harwood

The grey mists of November fail to dim the sparkling vivacity of the Hodder and Ribble rivers. The petrol-blue flash of a kingfisher slices through the dullness and the white bibs of a pair of dippers appear brilliant against the sombre winter weather. Nuthatches and tree creepers climb the fissured bark of oak, their antics unobscured by foliage. The days may be short and gloomy but the walk is one of the best in Lancashire.

Park in a large lay-by below the Higher Hodder Bridge Hotel, 3 miles west of Clitheroe. Cross the bridge over the wide, slow-flowing Hodder and turn left into the signposted footpath. Walk the tree-lined path deep into Hodder Woods. Oak, beech and elm clothe the steep slopes to the river as the path climbs, deeply covered with bronzed leaves.

Continue beside the chuckling river as the path moves out into pastures. Look for the heron hunched on a boulder midstream, patiently waiting for prey. A pair of dippers make use of another boulder to bob and preen. The path then moves into woodland once more. Notice the sturdy footbridges and the consolidation done to the footpath last year, making it a pleasure to walk.

At the waymark turn right to climb the many steps to an airy path that continues left, high above the river gorge. Here blue tits and long tailed tits flit through the branches of beech and a grey squirrel noisily scrambles through the tree tops. Continue down another flight of steps. At the bottom continue ahead to come close to the river once more. Stride up the cart-track, ignoring the dead-end footpath along the riverbank, to a stiled gate.

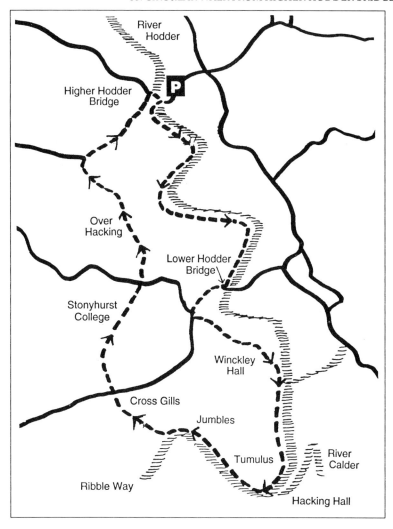

Walk ahead over pastures with the Hodder still flowing sweetly beside you. In a dead elm a nuthatch hammers at a seed, striking with its whole body as if its legs were hinged. Stroll beside the river as it makes a wide curve, passing through two stiled gates before reaching the B6243 at Lower Hodder Bridge. Stand on the three-arched bridge for a good view of the Old Hodder Bridge, built in 1562 by Richard Shireburn of Stonyhurst. It is generally called Cromwell Bridge and legend has it that Cromwell's troops crossed it at the time of the battle

133

of Preston.

Do not cross the Hodder but walk uphill (west) along the B6243, part of the Ribble Way, to a ladder stile on the left, opposite a bus shelter. Beyond, walk ahead to another waymarked stile, left of a small pond where mallards have already paired. Climb the slope ahead to walk beside a large plantation, on your left. Continue to the next waymark (broken) and bear right across the

pasture to pass through two kissing gates to a lane. Turn left.

Walk past Winckley Hall to Winckley Hall Farm, where once the duck pond powered a water wheel and where one of the beamed barns has aisles on both sides, adding more floor area to the building. Head on along the track following the waymarks. Just beyond where the track reaches the river, the Ribble joins the Hodder. By this glorious confluence, where grey wagtails disport, is the place for your lunch.

Stride on along the grassy way, beside

Heron and kingfisher by
Old Hodder Bridge

134

the wide surging Ribble. Redshanks give their haunting call as they fly upstream. Look right over the hedge to see two man-made mounds. In one were found Bronze Age remains. Follow the river as it makes a wide meander. Here the River Calder adds its waters to the stately Ribble. On the far bank, beyond the Calder, stands the magnificent Hacking Hall, a Jacobean house with many mullioned windows.

Follow the waymarked path past the derelict Boat House. This once housed the ferryman who took travellers across the Ribble, between Winckley and Hacking. Follow the waymarks through a stiled gate and on to a cart-track close to Jumbles Farm. Where the track swings right continue along the stiled Ribble Way beside the river, passing through two stiled gates. Turn right and walk to a gate ahead. Continue up the slope on an indistinct path. A stone cross stands on a mound to your left. The path joins a cart-track which leads to Cross Gills Farm. Walk along the access track to cross the B6243. Walk up the track ahead and follow it as it swings right in front of some cottages.

Continue along this track, which skirts the cricket fields of Stonyhurst College, the Roman Catholic boarding school. Away to the left stands the many towered mansion built by the Shireburn family, the work starting in the sixteenth century. Walk ahead to pass through a kissing gate to a paddock, and take another to continue along a track beside the school's rugby fields. Cross the road ahead and walk along the track opposite. Follow it as it swings left to Over Hacking. Pass the dwellings on the left and pass through the gate ahead. Keeping to the right of the hedge pass through two stiles and into woodland. After 100 yards, look for the solid stone-stepped stile in the wall.

Strike diagonally right across the pasture to pick up the cart-track to some farm buildings. Turn right and walk the reinforced track to a road called Birdy Brow. Turn right and walk down the quiet lane. Turn right at the junction and Higher Hodder Bridge lies to your right.

34: Circular walk from Downham

Distance:	6 miles
Time:	4 hours
Terrain:	Easy walking all the way - but lots of mud after rain
Map:	OS Pathfinder 669 SD 64/74 Clitheroe and Chipping

Downham, the village claimed to be east Lancashire's prettiest, sits on the slope of a limestone hill, close to a Roman road that linked York with Ribchester. Downham Hall, built in the sixteenth century, is the home of the Assheton family and through the centuries they have preserved the village, allowing nothing to mar its picturesque charm.

The walk starts from the unobtrusive free car park, with its excellent facilities and splendid view of the village. Note that there are no pylons to mar the beauty of the village; the cables have all been laid below ground. Turn left on leaving the car park. Do not cross the ancient bridge over the Downham Beck, the haunt of a large number of very tame ducks, but cross the Pendle Road and continue upstream to pass several delightful cottages whose gardens straddle the beck.

Pass through a gap stile at the end of the lane and walk to the far right corner to a gap stile beside a feeder stream. Continue beside the dancing water, which is now to your left, along the field edge, through Lancashire at its best. Climb the next stile, close to the beck, and follow the path as it passes below beech and ash. Cross a footbridge and walk the path, with the beck now to your right, to a gap stile out of the trees. Keep in the same general direction towards the attractive Clay House. Follow the footpath sign to keep to the left of the farm and continue to a stile beside a gate and then another in the wall ahead.

Beyond, turn right and walk through the farm and along the farm track to Pendle Road. Turn right and take the signposted footpath on the left to walk the track to Gerna Farm, which is tucked below the steep lower slopes of the whaleback of Pendle Hill (1,831ft high). To the right stands Gerna Hill, a reef-knoll, deposited millions of years ago when the area was below the sea. Where the farm access track swings right continue ahead through a metal gate and walk on to cross two stiles. Bear very slightly left over the next pasture to join a farm-track.

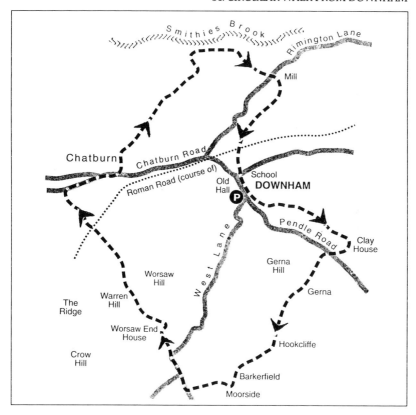

Pass through the gate and follow the track as it bears left. Bear left before the large barn, keeping to the left of Hookcliffe Farm (1714) to a stile onto the lower slopes of Pendle. Turn right to walk in front of a pleasing dwelling with mullioned windows. To the left, a hurrying stream descends the slopes in a series of sparkling waterfalls. Beyond the gate ahead you join the farm access track. After 300 yards, pass through a gate on the left of the way to walk a wide grassy shelf-like track. This leads to a footbridge over one more tumbling stream to a gate to Moorside Farm. Walk between the buildings to continue on the good track to a lane where you turn right. Ahead lies Worsaw Hill, another limestone reef-knoll.

On joining West Lane, continue ahead, and where it swings sharply right take the signposted gate in the hedge on your left. Stride on towards Worsaw End House. Beyond the gate, turn right and then bear

137

left, keeping left of the farm. Once beyond the metal barn take a gate on the right that leads to the lower slopes of Worsaw Hill. Climb the slope to join a wide grassy track and walk left. Above, the steep slopes are covered with scattered hawthorns and ash trees, and in many places the underlying limestone is exposed.

Look left for an extensive view of Pendle Hill. Keep level with the wall on your left, beyond which you can see the reef-knolls of Warren Hill, The Ridge and Crow Hill. Look at the stones of the wall for

Old stone bridge

the fossilised remains of thousands of branchipods and crinoids. Follow the path to the top of the slope where a magnificent view of rural, rolling Lancashire awaits.

Descend the slope to a gap stile and then continue down a steeper slope through holly, blackthorn and hawthorn to a stile in the far right corner of the wall. Stroll ahead towards a tall ash, crossing the course of the Roman road. Beyond, a stile gives access to the A59, which you cross with care. Drop down the public footpath on the other side to the stile and follow the grassy way, and then a path, to a stone stile. Cross a muddy track and take a second stile opposite. Continue ahead over a wide grassy sward with the hedge to your left and walk to the side of the beck, which you cross on stepping stones. Climb the signposted steps to walk ahead into Chatburn, where you turn right.

Stroll the charming main street, with its many attractive cottages, and continue across the high level bridge over the A59, from where you have more spectacular views. Cross the road and take the signposted stile to the left of a gate. Walk ahead along a track until you reach the boundary wall, where you bear right. Keep to the right of the hedge to walk an old trackway, now completely grassed over. Follow this to a stile and beyond walk the grassy tree-lined track. Pass through two gates to cross the railway line and stroll on, right, along the track. Beyond a gate, pass in front of a stone barn and turn left to pass through a gate.

Walk ahead from the gate and, on reaching the wooded slopes overlooking the wide, fast flowing Smithies Brook, turn right and continue high above the beck. Pass through a sturdy stile, cross a small footbridge and walk left to look at the fairy-tale packhorse bridge over the brook. Return from the bridge and walk beside woodland, now on your left, and take a muddy track swinging left. Continue beside the woodland and then pass below the gated railway bridge. Beyond, walk up the slope and look left to see a splendid stone viaduct. Walk on beside the larch plantation to Rimington Lane, which you cross, and then walk down the track opposite to view the old Downham corn mill on Ings Beck.

Return along the track and take the stile in the hedge on your left. Climb the slope, keeping to the right of the reef-knoll, which is topped with lofty beeches. Just before the brow, bear right and head for the top of the ridge and the top corner of the wood. Pause here for an astounding view ahead and behind you. Keeping close to the walled wood on your right, drop down to a step stile and walk on to take the gate on the right into Downham. Walk ahead to visit the church of St Leonard's, with its fifteenth century tower.

View of Downham

Continue down through the village, passing the stocks on your left and then the charming Steward's House, now three cottages. Cross the bridge and turn right to rejoin your car after a walk that has something interesting or exciting to view round every corner.

35: Circular walk from Eccleston via Croston

Distance:	5¹⁄₂ miles
Time:	3 hours
Terrain:	Easy walking. Farm tracks can be muddy
Map:	OS Pathfinder 699 SD 41/51 Chorley and Burscough Bridge

Start this walk at Eccleston, close to the church and the River Yarrow, perhaps one of the most peaceful scenes in south-west Lancashire. Stroll the gentle, low-lying pastures to Croston, the 'town of the cross'. Today's village cross was erected in 1950 on small steps in cobbled Church Street, a delightful terrace of cottages that frames the late-Gothic church of St Michael and All Angels.

Just north of the church, at the north end of Eccleston and beyond Eccleston Bridge, the road divides. Ignore the main branch, Lydiate Lane, and park on the left, in a grassy lay-by, 200 yards along New Lane. Walk on along the lane for another 200 yards, to turn left into an unsignposted farm-track, leading to a gate to Ingrave Farm. Follow the indistinct track as it swings right between farm buildings and then curves left along the outer edge of what is called a moat on the OS map. Climb a gate and continue on, with a hedge to the left, over rough pasture to a stile in the far left corner.

Carry on with the hedge to your left and the aptly named Spent Brook - it really does seem to have spent all its energy. Straddle the next stile, close to the brook. Follow the hedge round right to a stiled footbridge over a small tributary stream. Here a jay flies from a large oak, calling raucously, and beyond dozens of young rooks circle noisily over a pasture. Cross left over another footbridge and beyond turn right and then left to edge the pasture.

Turn right through the next gate and walk a grassy track with the hedge to your left, where fieldfare feast on the plentiful hawthorn berries. Climb the stile, left of the next gate, and walk on warily over a wet area between a derelict house and a barn. Pass through the next gate and follow the track, which steadily improves, towards Sarscow Farm. Walk the gated track to the left of the farm and press on along Sarscow

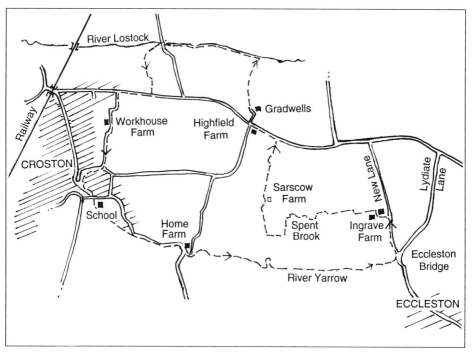

Lane. From the wide ditch to the right moorhens move off into the field. Blue tits chatter in the hazels and oaks about the water.

At the lane end, cross the A581 (Moor Road) and turn left to pass a caravan site and an old milestone. Turn right to take the signposted footpath opposite Highfield Road. Walk towards Gradwells Farm, where a grey squirrel dances through the leaves. Cross diagonally left over the car park of The Mill Hotel to a rustic arch over a gap in the boundary hedge at the left and behind the hotel.

Continue on the same diagonal to join a wide track, where you turn right to walk away from the hotel. Pass through a gate at the end of the track and head over the pasture to the side of the River Lostock. Turn left and walk beside the slowly flowing water, which is lined with reeds and shadowed by willows.

Climb the stile in the hawthorn hedge close to the river, where redwings fly off with quick flight as they are disturbed. Pass through a gate, cross a farm-track and climb the stile opposite. Walk diagonally right across the pasture to climb yet another stile and then walk ahead beside the hedge to your left. Pass through the wettest muddy gap in

141

Town Bridge, Croston with bluetit on hazel

Lancashire, climb through parallel poles that on the author's last visit to the area barred the right of way. Continue ahead, now with the hedge to your right, to a signposted stile to the B5249. Turn right and walk on to the signposted footpath leading left.

Step out along the reinforced path as it swings right and then left and becomes cobbled. Pass Workhouse Farm and stroll on to turn right into Out Lane, which leads to the centre of Croston. Look for the delightful

142

thatched cottage, dated 1705, on the right. Beyond the Lord Nelson pub, turn left into Town Road in the direction of the church.

To your right flows the River Yarrow, which is flanked with high walls and deep banks. It is crossed by the reinforced hump-backed Town Bridge, built in 1682. Do not cross but turn right into Church Street to pass the old forge and continue to the splendid old church. All round the building are ancient gravestones. To the right of St Michael's stands the fourteenth century school, licensed by John of Gaunt, Duke of Lancaster. If you wish to visit the church, you can obtain the key from the vicarage in Westhead Road. (It is kept locked after a disastrous burglary.) At this point you may wish to explore the village to see the several groups of almshouses and a farm in the main street.

To continue the walk, dawdle on beyond the church to head along a pleasing footpath with the Yarrow to your right. Climb the stile and follow the riverbank to take a stile on your left, beyond the last house on your left. The stile gives access to Grape Lane. Turn right and carry on past the gates to the avenue which once led to Croston Hall, home since the Middle Ages of the de Trafford family. When the last member of the line died, it was pulled down.

Head on to come beside the Yarrow once more, passing Home Farm. Turn left into the track, signposted Eccleston, just before Croston Mill Bridge. Take the stile ahead to continue beside the river and the mill weir, which once provided the power to turn the old mill wheel. Straddle the stile in the left corner of the field. Follow a tractor-rutted track (now with the hedge to your right) until the way leads through a gap (the hedge now on your left). The indistinct path swings right to the side of the delightfully meandering Yarrow with a fine view of the church at Eccleston ahead.

Continue over three stiles and then take a fourth to come to the side of the water. Then follow the way left to another stile to walk in front of several cottages, close to Eccleston Bridge. Turn left, and left again to rejoin your car.

36: Walk along the River Ribble starting from Gisburn

Distance:	8 miles
Time:	4-5 hours
Terrain:	Easy walking all the way, but walking boots advisable
Maps:	OS Pathfinder 670 SD 84/94 Barnoldswick and Earby
	669 SD 64/74 Clitheroe and Chipping

For much of this walk from Gisburn to Sawley, the way comes close to the stately River Ribble. Enjoy the splendid waterside path and the dramatic ruins of Salley (Sawley) Abbey. On your return pass through pastures where hazel hedges are laden with catkins and frolicsome lambs are forerunners of spring.

Leave the A59 at Gisburn by the lane signposted Bolton-by-Bowland. Two hundred yards along, on the railway bridge, park in a wide lay-by on the left. On the opposite side of the bridge, look over the parapet to see the ornate entrance to a tunnel. You may even see one of the occasional steam trains, emerging on its journey from Blackburn to Hellifield.

Walk on along the lane and turn left to join the signposted Ribble Way. At this point it is a public bridleway that traverses part of the access track to Copy House. Cross the cattle-grid, where a sign says that landowners welcome caring walkers. To the left lies Pendle Hill, its ridge covered in mist. Follow the Ribble Way sign and continue ahead where the track divides. Turn right in front of two dwellings to take a ladder stile over a fence. Walk ahead to cross two stiles to a gate that gives access to a mixed plantation. Walk the narrow path to a gate out of the trees.

Cross a footbridge over a small stream and turn right as directed by a waymark. Ascend the slope to the left to a waymark at the top of a narrow gill where blue tits chatter in hawthorns. Look for the waymark sign on a huge oak and then head for the waymarked stile to the right of the farm buildings. Cross to the reinforced track that leads to the farm and turn right to walk downhill into peaceful rolling pastures.

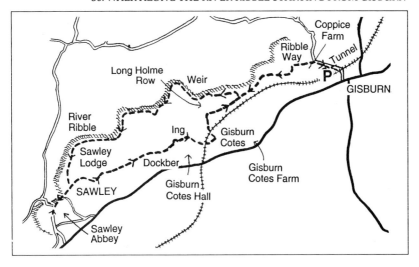

At the bottom of the hill, bear slightly left to a stile and a gate to continue along the Ribble Way. Walk past a field barn to take a stile on the right just beyond. Turn left and, keeping the hedge to the left, walk to the stile ahead. Stride on along the side of a huge pasture until the waymark directs you to the right just before a small stream. Note this point because this is where you rejoin the Ribble Way on your return.

Step out to a gate and beyond walk the path that runs above the glorious Ribble, where mallards swim and fly downstream. Owls call from the deciduous woodland that clothes the steep slopes of the opposite bank. The path leads down to the side of the river, now wide and shallow. Cross the stile and follow the path into a small gorge. Climb the stepped path through the beech trees, the path littered with dead leaves. Look for the lime-loving hart's tongue fern flourishing below the trees. The path is railed and takes you safely along the edge of a steep drop to the hurrying water.

Follow the path, which is bordered with primrose leaves, as it begins to descend towards the side of the river once more. The reinforced path, lined with alders, leads to a stile beyond which a heron fishes on a weir. Sit on the seat and enjoy this lovely corner of Lancashire.

Head on through the tree-lined valley, where coal tits and tree creepers attack the mossy bark of trees for insects. Climb the way, now a track, to pass through the trees. Then descend a continuing stepped path through alder and ash woodland. Beyond the next stile, cross a small stream and pass into an open area close beside the river. Follow the waymarked route through park-like pasture to a stile into a conifer plantation.

Beyond the conifers look for the stately beeches, the tangle of their roots exposed by the river when previously in spate. Walk on to a stile to more open pasture. Look for the next stile 50 yards to the left of the riverbank. Stride on slightly to left, keeping the fence to your left, over pastureland. A kestrel flies overhead and then hovers over the surprisingly lush grass. Climb the next stile and walk on.

Stride several footbridges over ditches and climb another stile. Then walk ahead, keeping the hedge to left. Long tailed tits pass through the branches and a green woodpecker calls. Look for a gated footbridge over a ditch on the left. Beyond, turn right and walk into Sawley.

Look right to see the splendid three-arched Sawley Bridge and continue past the Spread Eagle Hotel. Visit Salley Abbey, a Cistercian Abbey founded in 1148. Stroll the beautifully kept grass to view the dramatic ruins, rising into the sky with a grand backcloth of grassy hills and wooded slopes.

Return to walk the road towards Sawley Lodge. At the end of the buildings on the right, pass through a gate on the right and cross a narrow pasture to take a gate onto a farm lane. Turn left and walk uphill through more glorious countryside to pass in front of Dockber Cottage and Dockber Farm. Stride on along the farm-track, with an impressive view of the great whaleback of Pendle Hill to the right.

Pass through the gate and take the next immediately on the right. Head to the right corner of a small plantation and climb the fence to pass a roofless building on your right. Pass through a derelict gate and walk ahead beside the plantation. At the end of the trees continue through a gate a little to the right. Walk ahead to pass through another gate to an ancient track that leads to another gate. Turn left, and then, in front of Ing Farmhouse, turn right to walk its access road to a stile on the left. Walk ahead for another stile and then strike diagonally right to a gate to Gisburn Cotes Hall. The house has a huge outside chimney.

Walk ahead, keeping to the left of the farmhouse, to cross the bridge over the railway. Follow the track as it swings left to pass two large barns. Just before the next farm, Gisburn Cotes, take a gate on the left and walk ahead where Suffolk ewes have several rollicking lambs, to recross the railway using a grass-covered bridge. Bear right and follow the track to a stile in the left corner of the hedge to the left of several dwellings at Long Holme Row. Walk to pass through the gate ahead.

Turn right and pass in front of the dwellings and then walk left between farm buildings. Take the gate ahead and strike diagonally right to pass through a gate in the far corner of the pasture. Turn left and, keeping the hedge to the left, walk towards a stile. Do not cross but turn right and walk beside the fence and a few hedgerow trees on your left to a stile in the boundary ahead. Step across the ditch beyond and take the gate on the left to rejoin the Ribble Way. Turn right and retrace your outward journey.

Salley Abbey

37: Circular walk from Thornton

Distance:	5¹⁄₂ miles
Time:	3 hours
Terrain:	Easy walking all the way. Some unavoidable road walking
Map:	OS Pathfinder 658 SD 34/35 Fleetwood

The River Wyre rises in the Forest of Bowland, flowing through pleasing villages such as Scorton and St Michael's and passing close to Garstang and Poulton-Le-Fylde before discharging its water into the sea at Fleetwood. This 5¹⁄₂ mile circular walk starts at Marsh Mill village, Thornton, and continues beside the lovely river.

Park in Marsh Mill village, which is well signposted as you approach north along the B5268. Look for the centrepiece of the village, a windmill, its red sails high above the houses, to help you locate the site. The windmill was built in 1794 and was a working mill until 1922, grinding first flour and later meal. Marsh Mill gets its name from the marshy site on which it was originally built. Today the machinery has been restored and new sails fitted. Its lower two floors are open to all and you can go on a guided tour of the remainder for a small fee.

Stand with your back to The Tavern and walk diagonally left through the car park and into another car park behind the public library. Turn right to walk to the traffic lights and then left into the B5412, Victoria Road, in the direction of Thornton. Walk ahead, crossing the railway line and passing The Bay Horse public house. Where the road swings sharply right, walk ahead along Stanah Road. Then turn right into Raikes Road and walk the quiet rural way, where blackbirds and mistle thrushes feast upon hawthorn berries. Continue past old stables, named Abbeystead, still with a mounting block against a wall.

Take the waymarked stile on the left, signposted Woodhouse Road, just beyond an electricity sub-station. Walk ahead across a meadow to a stile in the opposite corner. Beyond, turn left and walk the access track, signposted Skippool and Stanah. Just before Thornton Hall Farm, turn right to climb a waymarked stile. Follow the waymarks to stride the field edge along two sides of a large pasture with a grand view of the Bowland hills ahead.

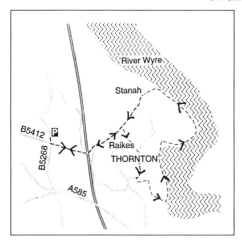

Climb the stile and bear right through willows and ash, where a flock of chaffinches flit through the branches, to the side of the River Wyre. Look right to see the Shard toll bridge and then turn left to take the track just beyond the road to the boat club. Keep to the river side of the clubhouse and, beyond, follow the signpost to enjoy the pleasing riverside walk. Out of the sandbanks crowd a large mixed flock of green plovers, gulls and redshanks. Continue past more than a hundred slatted jetties which stretch out to the water, most with boats moored.

To the left the path is shadowed by beech and hawthorn, the haunt of blue, great and long tailed tits. Beyond the moorings the track leads into the open countryside, with tidal gutters and salt marsh to the right and pastures to the left. Follow the riverside path as it swings right in the direction of Stanah and Cockle Hall. Look back for a picturesque view of the many boats moored on the estuary. Continue to a well placed seat - just right for your picnic and for watching the waders on the exposed mudflats. Here more redshanks and green plovers feed. Curlews and geese fly along the estuary, calling as they go. Shags move upriver, keeping close to the silvery water. Here too a dozen heron feed, only a few feet apart. Regularly, and seemingly deliberately, they fly over the smaller birds, putting them up in a noisy cloud.

Walk on along the path, with salt marsh to your right. Close to the water grows cord-grass, glasswort and marsh samphire but nearer to land flourishes sea aster, sea-purslane, sea-blite, sea lavender, sea arrowgrass and sea plantain. Continue to the site of an isolated tiny nineteenth century dwelling, known as Cockle Hall - named after a great cockle bed in the nearby river. Because it was so remote the original tenant, the father of 13 children, described himself as 'the only squire this side of the Wyre'. In 1989 the small site was developed and picnic tables were added so that it could be enjoyed by the disabled.

Ignore the footpath leading off on the left and walk on. Follow the

Sea heather, arrowhead grass and sea plantain

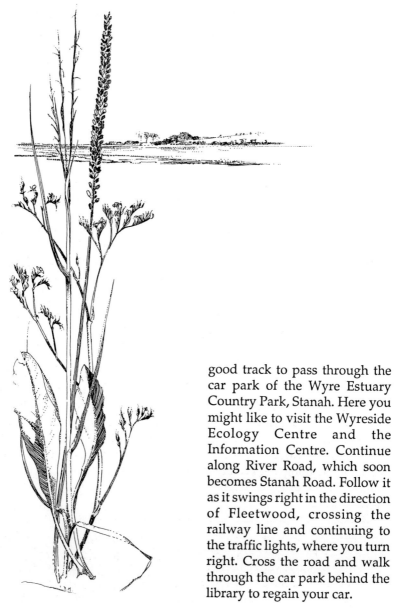

good track to pass through the car park of the Wyre Estuary Country Park, Stanah. Here you might like to visit the Wyreside Ecology Centre and the Information Centre. Continue along River Road, which soon becomes Stanah Road. Follow it as it swings right in the direction of Fleetwood, crossing the railway line and continuing to the traffic lights, where you turn right. Cross the road and walk through the car park behind the library to regain your car.

38: A circular walk from Worthington Lakes, through South Lancashire and along the Leeds and Liverpool Canal

Distance:	7½ miles
Time:	3-4 hours
Terrain:	Easy walking all the way
Map:	OS Pathfinder 699 SD 41/51 Chorley and Buscough Bridge

This walk starts and ends just beyond the county border and, in between, takes you over the quiet rolling pastures of south Lancashire.

Park in the large car park (not well signposted) of the nature reserve at North-West Water's Worthington Lakes (reservoirs). The lakes lie on the east side of Chorley Road (A5106), east of Standish. Leave the car park and walk right (north) along the A road. Turn left into a grassy track just before a dwelling called County House. Head straight across the continuing pasture to a footbridge into woodland. Follow the path as it swings right to pass through oak, rowan, sycamore and birch. As you approach the end of the woodland the path swings left and over pasture towards the railway line.

Turn right to join another path and walk on. Here two herons fly up from Bradley Brook and head off in the direction of the lakes. At the end of the path turn right and then walk left in front of a row of cottages. Turn right to walk down a narrow road until you reach The Crown public house where you turn sharp left to stride a reinforced track. Cross the iron bridge over the railway. Follow the track where it curves right and on along the 'Private road, farm only', ignoring the left turn. A mixed flock of gulls, starlings and green plovers feed in a newly ploughed field.

Recross the railway and walk towards Talbot House Farm. Follow the track right and then left through the outbuildings to walk a good track. Stride on for 50 yards beyond the hedge on your left, turn right to walk another 50 yards, then turn left to continue in the same general direction over a pasture to climb a stile that brings you to the right side of a hedge. Stroll on to a stile on your left, which you cross. Continue,

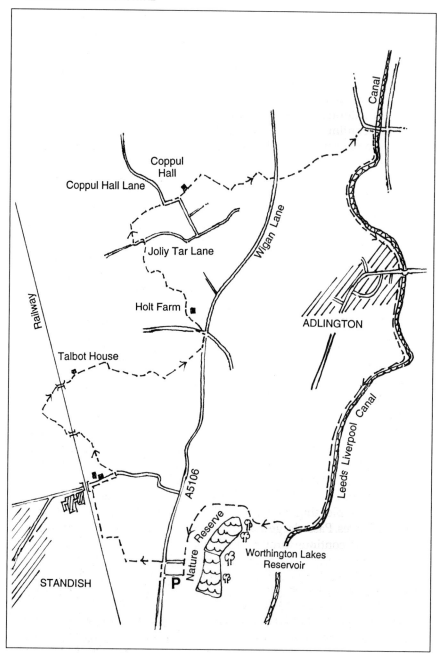

now with a hedge to your right, to a stile onto Chorley Road.

Walk left along the road to cross Coppull Mill Bridge and into Lancashire. Take the reinforced track on the left, beside willow, and continue beyond the gate. Pass the derelict Holt Farm on your right and walk on to a gate. The stile to take is before the gate on your left but barbed wire makes it difficult to climb. Beyond, walk ahead to a stranded stile on the edge of an attractive pond, in the right corner of the pasture. Continue ahead from the stile, and then turn left to edge the field to another stranded stile. Behind this is another, which you climb. Bear right and follow the hedge to a signposted stile to Jolly Tar Lane.

Turn left and then right to take the signposted track towards Highfield Farm. Look for the waymarks on the first barn and bear right into a gated muddy track. If the electric fence is across the track, negotiate it carefully, and walk beside the hawthorn hedge on the right to a signposted stile to Coppull Hall Lane.

Turn right and walk on. Take a waymarked track on the left, keeping to the right of a barn. Pass through a white gate and then keep to the right of a hedge and walk towards a beautiful beech laden with richly bronzed leaves. Pass through a gap at the end of the pasture and turn right to walk towards magnificent woodland, which clothes the site of a disused mine. Ignore the stile ahead and turn left to walk beside the colourful trees now to your right. Turn right to pass through a sturdy tunnel, all that remains of a railway that once passed below the glorious trees. Follow the continuing track left and, where the path divides, take the right branch to walk to Wigan Lane.

Cross the busy road with care and walk the signposted and stiled track ahead over pastures. A signposted exit beside a cottage called the Round House brings you to a road, which you cross. Turn right and then left onto the towpath of the Leeds and Liverpool Canal. Turn right to pass under the bridge, where you can see the grooves in the masonry caused by the ropes attached to the horses that pulled the boats. Stride on along the pleasing way, where the tranquil water is covered with autumn leaves. Pass a large marina, where dozens of colourful boats are moored, and continue through Adlington, passing under a bridge that has been widened to carry a road. Dawdle on into the lovely countryside and cross the enormously tall aqueduct over a picturesque stream far below. Just before the canal makes a sharp swing to the right you leave Lancashire for Greater Manchester.

Pass beneath a tall bridge and walk on. Ignore the footpath going off on the right and continue under the next bridge. Walk on along the glorious way to pass more glorious woodland. Carry on round a bend to the right and, just before it makes a swing to the left and immediately before the end of the trees, take an unsignposted wide track on the right. It passes below magnificent sycamores, beeches and then limes. Cross the footbridge over the River Douglas. Turn left and head on above the fast flowing river through the colourful woodland.

Straddle a stile onto a dam of one of the lakes. Continue over the embankment between two of the lakes, where coots idle on the water. Look here for several pairs of great crested grebes. These handsome birds swim fast on the water, with their slim necks stiffly erect, all the time uttering their soft calls. Continue left to walk beside the next lake, where you might see the flash of a kingfisher. Stroll past the next dam and the picnic table site, shuffling through the enormous carpet of leaves as you go, to return to the car park with its excellent facilities and to rejoin your car.

Oak and birch twigs, great crested grebe

154

39: Circular walk from Elswick, north-west of Preston

Distance:	7½ miles
Time:	3-4 hours
Terrain:	Easy walking, but after rain some of the field paths over the rich clay become sticky and soggy
Map:	OS Pathfinder 679 SD 43/53 Preston (North) and Kirkham (Lancs)

This walk through quiet pastures links farms with sturdy red brick farmhouses. In the thorn hedges ash and oak thrive, and now in winter their branches, bereft of leaves, reveal a pleasing symmetry. Most of the walk is on footpaths and Roseacre is the only village through which you pass. Enjoy this rich fertile area of Lancashire, once owned by Furness Abbey.

Park in the car park of the Boot and Shoe public house at Elswick, where the landlord welcomes walkers. Turn right (east) out of the pub and walk along the road. Where it swings sharp right, walk on to pass Bonds, an ice cream parlour and refreshment bar. Continue down the lovely lane, past Ash Farm and out into the peaceful countryside. Take the signposted footpath on the left, from where there is a magnificent view of the brooding Bowland Fells. Walk the wide grassy way to a metal gate. Beyond, cross the next pasture to climb a stile in the opposite hedge. Strike diagonally left to cross a ditch by a plank to walk ahead, with the fence and ditch to your left. Ignore the footbridge on your left and carry on over the footbridge ahead.

Head on, bearing to the right of two willow fringed ponds. They were possibly marl pits, from which clay for brick-making was removed. Look for the narrow, muddy path between the second and a third pond and straddle a stile in the hedge on your left. Bear right to follow the hedge on your right, passing the third pond, where paired mallards take flight. Continue past a small copse, the tall trees reflecting clearly in the deep water below. Stroll on past another pit of water, shadowed by tall ash and surrounded by alders. Walk on to the lane ahead,

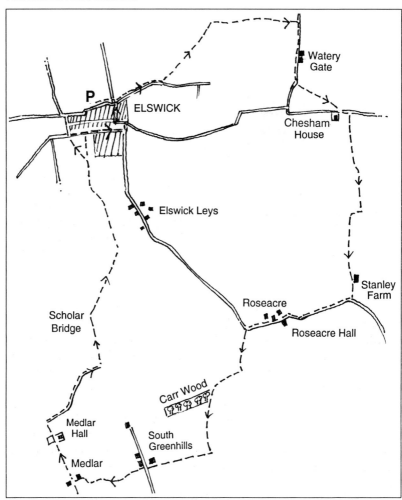

enjoying a dramatic view of Pendle Hill.

Turn right to walk the hedged way to pass Watery Gate Farm. Then take a signposted footpath on the left, under an ash, just before the Elswick Manor. Head on to pass two more ponds on your left and continue to the signposted white gate in front of the red brick Chesham House Farm. Turn left to pass the farm and straddle the signposted stile on the right to walk ahead, with the fence to your left and the farm to your right. Climb the next stile with the hedge still to your left. The next stile brings you to the left of the continuing hedge. Walk on the stiled

Elswick Church

way through fields to a footbridge over a narrow dyke. Beyond, turn right to walk the parish boundary.

After a hundred yards, turn left to strike across the pasture to a stiled gate to a farm track to Stanley Farm. Here waymarks direct you through the outbuildings to the access track beyond. At the lane, turn right to walk the hedged way to the small village of Roseacre, which seems to be a village of farms with a few houses between them. Stroll on beyond the dwellings to take the unsignposted second gate on the left after the last house on the left. Strike slightly right across the pasture, where a large hare lopes off out of sight, to continue beside the hedge now on your right. Follow it right to take the metal gate directly ahead (ignore the gate on your right).

Beyond keep beside the hedged and fenced ditch on your right to pass two ponds where willow and reedmace thrive and moorhens hurry into the yellowing vegetation. Strike diagonally left to pass through the gate at the left corner of Carr Wood, where a kestrel hovers. Continue on the same left diagonal across the next rather wet pasture to cross a stiled footbridge over Scholar Beck, a narrow brown stream deep in its cutting.

Turn left and immediately cross a rough ditch where you turn right to walk uphill. Pass through a gap in the hedge ahead and then stride on to pass through a gate. Ignore the access track on the right to South

157

Greenhills and walk on, keeping to left of the wire fence, to climb a stile close to the garden hedge of the farm. It can be very wet here and you may need to make a small diversion. Turn right to step out to a gate, beyond which you turn left. Stroll the narrow hedged lane to pass a semi-circular copse. Follow the lane as it swings right to pass the red brick Leyland Hall Farm.

Where the lane makes a sharp turn left, press ahead to walk past Medlar Hall Farm, climbing two stiles to carry on along a hedged track into the countryside. Continue where the track swings right and where it makes several small zig-zags and becomes pitted and wet. When the hedge ceases on the left, follow the hedge on your right to a footbridge over a narrow dyke, where a heron flies off. Do not cross the bridge, but turn left and walk beside the long straight water channel to cross the sturdy Scholar Bridge over Scholar Beck once again.

Walk right to the hedge and dyke to your right and stride beside them to the top right corner of this huge pasture. Ahead you can see the huge silo of Elswick Leys Farm, with the church tower to its left. Bear left to a stile and beyond walk ahead with the hedge to your right. Pass through the very narrow gap stile to the right of the gate. Stride on past the farm, with the silo to your right, to a footbridge across a dyke, half way along the boundary hedge ahead of you. Continue with the hedge to your right towards some newish houses. Follow the hedge round to the left to a gap stile. Beyond, continue beside the hedge to your right to climb a stile on the right.

Stride on along a ginnel that passes between the houses and follow it until it ends at Roseacre Lane. Turn left and then right into Lodge

Lane. From here there is a picturesque view of Elswick Congregational Church. It was built in 1873 and looks as if it ought to be the parish church. The sturdy tower sits squarely in the middle of the building and then becomes elegantly octagonal as it tapers upward.

Return along Lodge Lane to the crossroads, then turn right and follow the road round to rejoin your car.

Moorhen

CICERONE GUIDES

Cicerone publish a wide range of reliable guides to walking and climbing in Britain, and other general interest books.

LAKE DISTRICT - General Books
CONISTON COPPER A History
CHRONICLES OF MILNTHORPE
A DREAM OF EDEN
THE HIGH FELLS OF LAKELAND
LAKELAND - A taste to remember (Recipes)
LAKELAND VILLAGES
LAKELAND TOWNS
THE LOST RESORT? (Morecambe)
LOST LANCASHIRE (Furness area)
OUR CUMBRIA Stories of Cumbrian Men and Women
THE PRIORY OF CARTMEL
REFLECTIONS ON THE LAKES
AN ILLUSTRATED COMPANION INTO LAKELAND

LAKE DISTRICT - Guide Books
THE BORDERS OF LAKELAND
BIRDS OF MORECAMBE BAY
CASTLES IN CUMBRIA
CONISTON COPPER MINES Field Guide
THE CUMBRIA CYCLE WAY
THE EDEN WAY
IN SEARCH OF WESTMORLAND
SHORT WALKS IN LAKELND-1: SOUTH LAKELAND
SCRAMBLES IN THE LAKE DISTRICT
MORE SCRAMBLES IN THE LAKE DISTRICT
WALKING ROUND THE LAKES
WALKS IN SILVERDALE/ARNSIDE
WESTMORLAND HERITAGE WALK
WINTER CLIMBS IN THE LAKE DISTRICT

NORTHERN ENGLAND (outside the Lakes
BIRDWATCHING ON MERSEYSIDE
CANAL WALKS Vol 1 North
CANOEISTS GUIDE TO THE NORTH EAST
THE CLEVELAND WAY & MISSING LINK
THE DALES WAY
DOUGLAS VALLEY WAY
WALKING IN THE FOREST OF BOWLAND
HADRIANS WALL Vol 1 The Wall Walk
HERITAGE TRAILS IN NW ENGLAND
THE ISLE OF MAN COASTAL PATH
IVORY TOWERS & DRESSED STONES (Follies)
THE LANCASTER CANAL
LANCASTER CANAL WALKS
A WALKERS GUIDE TO THE LANCASTER CANAL
LAUGHS ALONG THE PENNINE WAY
A NORTHERN COAST-TO-COAST
NORTH YORK MOORS Walks
THE REIVERS WAY (Northumberland)
THE RIBBLE WAY
ROCK CLIMBS LANCASHIRE & NW
WALKING DOWN THE LUNE
WALKING IN THE SOUTH PENNINES
WALKING IN THE NORTH PENNINES
WALKING IN THE WOLDS
WALKS IN THE YORKSHIRE DALES (3 VOL)
WALKS IN LANCASHIRE WITCH COUNTRY
WALKS IN THE NORTH YORK MOORS
WALKS TO YORKSHIRE WATERFALLS (2 vol)
WATERFALL WALKS -TEESDALE & THE HIGH PENNINES
WALKS ON THE WEST PENNINE MOORS
WALKING NORTHERN RAILWAYS (2 vol)
THE YORKSHIRE DALES A walker's guide

Also a full range of EUROPEAN and OVERSEAS guidebooks - walking, long distance trails, scrambling, ice-climbing, rock climbing.

DERBYSHIRE & EAST MIDLANDS
KINDER LOG
HIGH PEAK WALKS
WHITE PEAK WAY
WHITE PEAK WALKS - 2 Vols
WEEKEND WALKS IN THE PEAK DISTRICT
THE VIKING WAY
THE DEVIL'S MILL / WHISTLING CLOUGH (Novels)

WALES & WEST MIDLANDS
ASCENT OF SNOWDON
WALKING IN CHESHIRE
CLWYD ROCK
HEREFORD & THE WYE VALLEY A Walker's Guide
HILLWALKING IN SNOWDONIA
HILL WALKING IN WALES (2 Vols)
THE MOUNTAINS OF ENGLAND & WALES Vol 1 WALES
WALKING OFFA'S DYKE PATH
THE RIDGES OF SNOWDONIA
ROCK CLIMBS IN WEST MIDLANDS
SARN HELEN Walking Roman Road
SCRAMBLES IN SNOWDONIA
SNOWDONIA WHITE WATER SEA & SURF
THE SHROPSHIRE HILLS A Walker's Guide
WALKING DOWN THE WYE
WELSH WINTER CLIMBS

SOUTH & SOUTH WEST ENGLAND
WALKING IN THE CHILTERNS
COTSWOLD WAY
COTSWOLD WALKS (3 VOLS)
WALKING ON DARTMOOR
WALKERS GUIDE TO DARTMOOR PUBS
EXMOOR & THE QUANTOCKS
THE KENNET & AVON WALK
LONDON THEME WALKS
AN OXBRIDGE WALK
A SOUTHERN COUNTIES BIKE GUIDE
THE SOUTHERN-COAST-TO-COAST
SOUTH DOWNS WAY & DOWNS LINK
SOUTH WEST WAY - 2 Vol
THE TWO MOORS WAY Dartmoor-Exmoor
WALKS IN KENT Bk 2
THE WEALDWAY & VANGUARD WAY

SCOTLAND
THE BORDER COUNTRY - WALKERS GUIDE
BORDER PUBS & INNS A Walker's Guide
CAIRNGORMS WINTER CLIMBS
WALKING THE GALLOWAY HILLS
THE ISLAND OF RHUM
THE SCOTTISH GLENS (Mountainbike Guide)
  Book 1:THE CAIRNGORM GLENS
  Book 2 THE ATHOLL GLENS
  Book 3 THE GLENS OF RANNOCH
SCOTTISH RAILWAY WALKS
SCRAMBLES IN LOCHABER
SCRAMBLES IN SKYE
SKI TOURING IN SCOTLAND
TORRIDON A Walker's Guide
WALKS from the WEST HIGHLAND RAILWAY
WINTER CLIMBS BEN NEVIS & GLENCOE

REGIONAL BOOKS UK & IRELAND
THE ALTERNATIVE PENNINE WAY
CANAL WALKS Vol.1: North
LIMESTONE - 100 BEST CLIMBS
THE PACKHORSE BRIDGES OF ENGLAND
THE RELATIVE HILLS OF BRITAIN
THE MOUNTAINS OF ENGLAND & WALES
  VOL 1 WALES, VOL 2 ENGLAND
THE MOUNTAINS OF IRELAND

Other guides are constantly being added to the Cicerone List. Available from bookshops, outdoor equipment shops or direct (send s.a.e. for price list) from
CICERONE, 2 POLICE SQUARE, MILNTHORPE, CUMBRIA, LA7 7PY

PRINTED BY ST EDMUNDSBURY PRESS, BURY ST EDMUNDS, SUFFOLK